NATIONAL COOPERATIVE TRANSIT RESEARCH & DEVELOPMENT PROGRAM

2 Synthesis of Transit Practice

Enforcement of Priority Treatment for Buses on Urban Streets

JOHN J. ROARK
PAWA, Inc.
Dallas, Texas

Topic Panel

RON BOROWSKI, *Henningson, Durham & Richardson*
DONALD H. CARR, *Seattle Engineering Department*
MICHAEL A. REPLOGLE, *Public Technology, Inc.*
SAMUEL SCHWARTZ, *New York City Department of Transportation*
ROBERT E. SPICHER, *Transportation Research Board*
PAUL TAYLOR, *Los Angeles County Transportation Commission*
JAMES K. WILLIAMS, *Transportation Research Board*
DAVID K. WITHEFORD, *Transportation Research Board*
JAMES WIESEHUEGEL, *Dallas Transit System*

RESEARCH SPONSORED BY THE URBAN MASS TRANSIT ADMINISTRATION OF THE U.S. DEPARTMENT OF TRANSPORTATION

TRANSPORTATION RESEARCH BOARD
National Research Council
Washington, D.C. May 1982

NATIONAL COOPERATIVE TRANSIT RESEARCH & DEVELOPMENT PROGRAM

Administrators, engineers, and many others in the transit industry are faced with a multitude of complex problems that range between local, regional, and national in their prevalence. How they might be solved is open to a variety of approaches; however, it is an established fact that a highly effective approach to problems of widespread commonality is one in which operating agencies join cooperatively to support, both in financial and other participatory respects, systematic research that is well designed, practically oriented, and carried out by highly competent researchers. As problems grow rapidly in number and escalate in complexity, the value of an orderly, high-quality cooperative endeavor likewise escalates.

Recognizing this in light of the many needs of the transit industry at large, the Urban Mass Transportation Administration, U.S. Department of Transportation, got under way in 1980 the National Cooperative Transit Research & Development Program (NCTRP). This is an objective national program that provides a mechanism by which UMTA's principal client groups across the nation can join cooperatively in an attempt to solve near-term public transportation problems through applied research, development, test, and evaluation. The client groups thereby have a channel through which they can directly influence a portion of UMTA's annual activities in transit technology development and deployment. Although present funding of the NCTRP is entirely from UMTA's Section 6 funds, the planning leading to inception of the Program envisioned that UMTA's client groups would join ultimately in providing additional support, thereby enabling the Program to address a large number of problems each year.

The NCTRP operates by means of agreements between UMTA as the sponsor and (1) the National Academy of Sciences, a private, nonprofit institution, as the Primary Technical Contractor (PTC) responsible for administrative and technical services, (2) the American Public Transit Association, responsible for operation of a Technical Steering Group (TSG) comprised of representatives of transit operators, local government officials, State DOT officials, and officials from UMTA's Office of Technology Development and Deployment, and (3) the Urban Consortium for Technology Initiatives/Public Technology, Inc., responsible for providing the local government officials for the Technical Steering Group.

Research programs for the NCTRP are developed annually by the Technical Steering Group, which identifies key problems, ranks them in order of priority, and establishes programs of projects for UMTA approval. Once approved, they are referred to the National Academy of Sciences for acceptance and administration through the Transportation Research Board.

Research projects addressing the problems referred from UMTA are defined by panels of experts established by the Board to provide technical guidance and counsel in the problem areas. The projects are advertised widely for proposals, and qualified agencies are selected on the basis of research plans offering the greatest probabilities of success. The research is carried out by these agencies under contract to the Academy, and administration and surveillance of the contract work are the responsibilities of the Academy and Board.

The needs for transit research are many, and the National Cooperative Transit Research & Development Program is a mechanism for deriving timely solutions for transportation problems of mutual concern to many responsible groups. In doing so, the Program operates complementary to, rather than as a substitute for or duplicate of, other transit research programs.

NCTRP SYNTHESIS 2

Project 60-1 FY 1980 (Topic TS-2)
ISSN 0732-1856
ISBN 0-309-03415-9
Library of Congress Catalog Card No. 82-60315

Price: $6.40

Subject Areas
Planning
Energy and Environment
Transportation Safety
Operations and Traffic Control
Traffic Flow, Capacity, and Measurements

Modes
Highway Transportation
Public Transit

Published reports of the

NATIONAL COOPERATIVE TRANSIT RESEARCH & DEVELOPMENT PROGRAM

are available from:

Transportation Research Board
National Academy of Sciences
2101 Constitution Avenue, N.W.
Washington, D.C. 20418

Printed in the United States of America.

PREFACE

A vast storehouse of information exists on nearly every subject of concern to the transit industry. Much of this information has resulted from both research and the successful application of solutions to the problems faced by practitioners in their daily work. Because previously there has been no systematic means for compiling such useful information and making it available to the entire transit community, the Urban Mass Transportation Administration of the U.S. Department of Transportation has, through the mechanism of the National Cooperative Transit Research & Development Program, authorized the Transportation Research Board to undertake a series of studies to search out and synthesize useful knowledge from all available sources and to prepare documented reports on current practices in the subject areas of concern.

This synthesis series reports on various practices, making specific recommendations where appropriate but without the detailed directions usually found in handbooks or design manuals. Nonetheless, these documents can serve similar purposes, for each is a compendium of the best knowledge available on measures found to be successful in resolving specific problems. The extent to which these reports are useful will be tempered by the user's knowledge and experience in the particular problem area.

FOREWORD

By Staff
Transportation Research Board

This synthesis report will be useful to transit operators, transportation planners, traffic engineers, and others concerned with bus operations and traffic control in urban areas. Detailed information is presented on the role of enforcement in the successful operation of programs for priority treatment of buses on urban streets.

Administrators, engineers, and researchers are continually faced with problems on which much information exists, either in the form of reports or in terms of undocumented experience and practice. Unfortunately, this information often is scattered and unevaluated, and, as a consequence, in seeking solutions, full information on what has been learned about a problem frequently is not assembled. Costly research findings may go unused, valuable experience may be overlooked, and full consideration may not be given to the available methods of solving or alleviating the problem. In an effort to correct this situation, NCTRP Project 60-1, carried out by the Transportation Research Board as the research agency, has the objective of reporting on common transit problems and synthesizing available information. The synthesis reports from this endeavor constitute an NCTRP publication series in which various forms of relevant information are assembled into single, concise documents pertaining to specific problems or sets of closely related problems.

Various priority treatment techniques are used for buses on freeways and arterials. Enforcement has been found to be an important factor in the success of these efforts, but is frequently not given adequate attention in bus priority strategies for urban streets. This report of the Transportation Research Board presents information on the role of enforcement in bus priority operations and recommends enforcement measures and design guidelines.

To develop this synthesis in a comprehensive manner and to ensure inclusion of significant knowledge, the Board analyzed available information assembled from numerous sources, including a large number of public transportation agencies. A topic panel of experts in the subject area was established to guide the researcher in organizing and evaluating the collected data, and to review the final synthesis report.

This synthesis is an immediately useful document that records practices that were acceptable within the limitations of the knowledge available at the time of its preparation. As the processes of advancement continue, new knowledge can be expected to be added to that now at hand.

CONTENTS

NOTICE

ACKNOWLEDGMENTS

This synthesis was completed by the Transportation Research Board under the supervision of Paul E. Irick, Assistant Director for Special Technical Activities Division. The Principal Investigators responsible for conduct of the synthesis were Thomas L. Copas and Herbert A. Pennock, Special Projects Engineers. This synthesis was edited by Nancy A. Ackerman.

Special appreciation is expressed to John J. Roark, Vice President, PAWA, Inc., Dallas, Texas, who was responsible for the collection of data and the preparation of the report.

Valuable assistance in the preparation of this synthesis was provided by the Topic Panel, consisting of Ron Borowski, Manager, Transportation Planning and Engineering, Henningson, Durham & Richardson; Donald H. Carr, Acting Manager X, Seattle Engineering Department; Michael A. Replogle, Public Technology, Inc.; Samuel Schwartz, Assistant Commissioner, New York City Department of Transportation; Paul Taylor, Deputy Executive Director for Programming and Fiscal Analysis, Los Angeles County Transportation Commission; and James Wiesehuegel, Assistant General Manager for Administration, Dallas Transit System.

Robert E. Spicher, Projects Engineer, James K. Williams, Transportation Safety Coordinator, and David K. Witheford, Engineer of Traffic and Operations, of the Transportation Research Board, assisted the Project 60-1 Staff and the Topic Panel.

Information on current practice was provided by many transit agencies. Their cooperation and assistance were most helpful.

ENFORCEMENT OF PRIORITY TREATMENT FOR BUSES ON URBAN STREETS

SUMMARY

More efficient use of buses primarily consists of providing priority treatment for buses on freeways and arterials. Successful bus priority treatment has resulted in reduced travel time for buses, improved schedule reliability, increased transit ridership and, in many instances, improved traffic conditions within the travel corridor.

An evaluation of both successful and unsuccessful bus priority efforts has identified the importance of enforcement in bus priority strategies. A less than adequate enforcement effort has often tended to reduce public respect for the priority treatment and has thus significantly reduced its effectiveness. Also significant has been the lack of consideration given to enforcement during the design of the project. Although bus priority schemes often require substantial changes to traffic patterns and result in unintentional violations by motorists, law enforcement officers have not been involved in the project design and have only been called in when lack of enforcement jeopardizes the success of the project.

Police agencies have generally viewed enforcement of bus priority projects as deserving less attention than crime prevention and investigation. There also has been some reluctance on the part of the courts to prosecute violations of nontraditional traffic measures.

The cost of enforcement measures, a lack of understanding of objectives, the absence of a clear organizational responsibility for enforcement, and often a facility and operational design that defy enforcement all have contributed to the enforcement problem. Emphasis must be placed on project designs that recognize the importance of enforcement of priority treatment for buses, support enforcement measures, and encourage self enforcement.

Priority treatment for buses on urban streets generally involves the use of buses on arterial facilities that have limited access from abutting property and permit off-peak turning movements. Enforcement becomes a major consideration when other roadway functions are restricted in favor of the bus. Project design must recognize the importance as well as the expense of enforcement, and incorporate features in the design to encourage self enforcement. Design guidelines are presented for (a) concurrent-flow bus lanes, (b) contraflow bus lanes, (c) bus-only and automobile-restricted zones, and (d) signal preemption. However, project design cannot substitute for a total program of enforcement, which includes extensive coordination and cooperation among the agencies involved in planning, designing, operating and enforcing the project, public education programs, use of traditional and nontraditional enforcement techniques, and establishment of adequate penalties for violators.

CHAPTER ONE

INTRODUCTION

PRIORITY TREATMENT FOR BUSES

Bus travel has been and is projected to be the major component of public transportation in the United States. National ridership figures for public transportation in 1980 indicated that 70 percent of the total transit daily trips were made by bus (*1*). Since 1975 major capital investments for urban transportation systems have been discouraged in favor of transportation system management (TSM) efforts to make the existing transportation system more effective. This improvement of urban transportation in most cities will mean increased reliance on bus systems and thus require more efficient use of buses in the total transportation system.

Using buses more efficiently primarily entails providing priority treatment for buses on freeways and arterials. Priority treatment has taken the form of (a) exclusive bus lanes on both freeways and arterials, (b) bus-only streets and automobile-free zones in the urban street network, and (c) signal preemption capability for buses. Each type of bus priority measure has been used successfully in the United States, and major successes have provided excellent examples of good design and operation as well as documentation of the benefits of bus priority treatment (Figure 1).

Successful bus priority treatment has resulted in reduced travel time for buses, improved schedule reliability, increased transit ridership, and, in many instances, improved traffic and safety conditions within the travel corridor. For example, on the Shirley Highway (I-95) high-occupancy vehicle (HOV) lanes in Washington, D.C. (Figure 2), bus reliability (arrival within 6 min of the scheduled time) increased from 33 percent before the bus priority treatment to 92 percent after implementation (*2*). On the Miami South Dixie Highway bus lane, an example of concurrent-flow priority treatment on an urban arterial, transit travel times were reduced by 5 to 10 min over a 5.5-mile segment (*3, 4*). In contraflow lanes on central business district (CBD) streets in Minneapolis, bus travel times were reduced by 20 percent and transit ridership increased by 7 percent, while automobile traffic showed no deterioration (*5*).

IMPORTANCE OF ENFORCEMENT

An evaluation of both the successful and unsuccessful bus priority programs has identified the importance of enforcement in bus priority strategies (*6*). A less than adequate enforcement effort often reduces public respect for the priority treatment and thus significantly reduces its effectiveness. The cost of enforcement, a lack of understanding of its objectives, the absence of a clear organizational responsibility for enforcement, and often a facility and operational design that defy enforcement all have contributed to the problems of enforcement efforts. For example, on a preferential HOV lane with little enforcement on a major freeway in Miami, the violation rate was over 75 percent (75 percent of the vehicles using the preferential lane were doing so illegally). In a self-enforcing preferential lane in Boston, the violation rate was over 80 percent.

Lack of emphasis on enforcement has been due in part to little concern on the part of transportation planners. Planning emphasis has traditionally been placed on facilities for longer urban trips, and enforcement of priority measures to facilitate shorter trips has been considered the responsibility of police agencies (*7*). Although bus priority schemes often require significant changes to traffic patterns and result in

FIGURE 1 Bus-only lanes in Portland, Oregon. *(Courtesy of American Public Transit Association.)*

FIGURE 2 Shirley Highway (I-95) HOV express lanes in Washington, D.C. (middle lanes are reserved exclusively for buses and carpools).

unintentional violations by motorists, law enforcement officers have not been involved in the project design and have only been called in when lack of enforcement jeopardizes the success of the project.

Police agencies have generally viewed enforcement of bus priority projects as deserving a lower priority than crime prevention and investigation and other types of traffic law enforcement. Budget constraints in both police agencies and transit authorities have limited the number of staff members that can be assigned to enforce bus priority projects. Also, the efficiency of police agencies has been hampered by reluctance of the courts to prosecute violators of nontraditional traffic measures. In many instances, the courts have required the apprehension of the violator for the serving of a citation, rejecting the validity of summons issued to violators identified by photography and license plates.

The lack of consideration of enforcement strategies during the design of a project has been a significant limitation of the enforcement effort; improper project design for bus priority treatment has often resulted in either expensive enforcement or an operation in which enforcement is difficult or impossible. Emphasis must be placed on project design and design characteristics that encourage self enforcement. Design guidelines that recognize the importance of enforcement, particularly self-enforcing characteristics, have only recently been given proper attention; however, more emphasis has been placed on bus priority treatment on freeways than on priority treatment on urban streets, even though operation and enforcement of bus priority treatment on urban arterials is significantly more difficult than on freeways because of cross-street volumes, turning movements, illegal parking, and access to abutting land uses.

PURPOSE OF SYNTHESIS

The importance of enforcement in various categories of bus priority treatment on urban streets is discussed in this report, along with suggested enforcement measures, and design characteristics of bus priority treatment by project type. The purpose of this synthesis is to provide transportation planners, traffic engineers, and transit operators with information on bus priority design guidelines in which enforcement is considered to be a primary element in a project's success.

REFERENCES

1. American Public Transit Association. *The Transit Fact Book.* Washington, D.C. (1981)
2. McQueen, J. T., D. M. Levinson, R. Waksman, and G. K. Miller. *Evaluation of the Shirley Highway Express-Bus-on-Freeway Demonstration Project.* Final Report for the National Bureau of Standards (1975)
3. Rose, H. S., and D. H. Hinds. South Dixie Highway Contraflow Bus and Carpool Lane Demonstration Project. Pp. 8–22 in *Transportation Research Record 606: Bus Transportation Strategies.* Transportation Research Board, Washington, D.C. (1976)
4. Rothenberg, M. J. *Priority Treatment for High Occupancy Vehicles: Project Status Report.* Prepared for the Federal Highway Administration by JHK & Associates (1977)
5. Minneapolis Public Works Department, Traffic Engineering Division. *Reverse Flow Bus Lanes: Second and Marquette Avenues.* Final Report. (1975)
6. Transportation Research Board. *NCHRP Synthesis 81: Experiences in Transportation System Management.* Washington, D.C. (1981) 88 pp.
7. Meyer, M. D., and J. Sheldon-Dean. *The Role of Enforcement in Short-Range Transportation Planning.* Center for Transportation Studies, Massachusetts Institute of Technology (1980)

CHAPTER TWO

ENFORCEMENT AND BUS PRIORITY TREATMENT

Bus priority measures, by design and definition, attempt to segregate traffic flows and give priority treatment to buses and other high-occupancy vehicles, often to the detriment of driver-only automobiles. Enforcement becomes a significant problem when automobile drivers are restricted from faster lanes, convenient turning movements, and on-street parking and are required to interpret and react to new or different traffic maneuvers. Since the transit operator and other agencies or departments are involved to an extent not required in routine traffic operations, enforcement of bus priority treatment requires extensive interagency coordination and cooperation. The agencies involved in planning, designing, implementing, and enforcing bus priority strategies often envision different objectives in enforcement and certainly give different weight to the importance of enforcement.

STATE OF THE ART OF BUS PRIORITY TREATMENT AND ENFORCEMENT

Planning and design practices for bus priority treatment were developed in 1975 by the Transportation Research Board under the National Cooperative Highway Research Program. *NCHRP Report 155: Bus Use of Highways, Planning and Design Guidelines* (*1*) serves as an excellent reference document for bus priority treatment on urban arterial facilities as well as on freeways and for terminals and transportation centers. The reader is encouraged to use this document as reference material for facility design.

In 1977, under the sponsorship of the U.S. Department of Transportation, Public Technology, Inc., developed a manual on planning and implementing priority techniques for high-occupancy vehicles (HOV) (*2*). Emphasis was placed on comprehensive procedures for various HOV techniques, and an enforcement plan was recommended as a part of project planning.

In 1978 the Federal Highway Administration published a report on enforcement requirements for HOV facilities that suggested procedures for the development of enforcement programs and enforcement guidelines for the design of HOV facilities (*3*). Guidelines and requirements were provided for both freeway and arterial HOV facilities.

The development of enforcement techniques for bus priority treatment has not paralleled the development of design guidelines. In evaluating enforcement in TSM planning, Meyer et al. (*4*) reported that "very few TSM planners considered enforcement during the planning process." Also noted was the hesitancy of police officers to enforce preferential bus (and HOV) lanes due to concern for the safety of the police officer, lack of resources for enforcement, and lack of involvement of the police agency in the project design phase.

Further evaluation is needed of the enforcement techniques and strategies that have been successfully employed in bus priority treatment. Design procedures that recognize the importance of self enforcement in bus priority measures and provide for simple yet effective monitoring must be disseminated for advancement in enforcement techniques.

Attention should also be directed to strategies and procedures for accomplishing the interagency coordination for enforcement in both the design and operational phases of bus priority treatment. This latter thrust demands an understanding of the participants involved in bus priority treatment and their attitudes toward enforcement.

PARTICIPANTS AND ATTITUDES IN BUS PRIORITY ENFORCEMENT

Bus priority treatment must bring together diverse agencies and disciplines in a creative manner for the development of objectives and approaches to enforcement. A significant factor in the enforcement of bus priority treatment is the number of agencies and other participants that must function in a well-coordinated effort for enforcement to be successful. The institutionalized procedures and objectives that each agency brings to this effort tend to segregate instead of coordinate enforcement activities.

In addition to the agencies involved in design and operation of bus priority projects, special interest groups and the general public react to and develop attitudes of compliance or noncompliance with project restrictions. An understanding of the attitudes of the participating agencies, interest groups, and the public is important in the development of a successful enforcement program.

Police Officials

Police agencies are organized in a paramilitary structure with strong authority and organizational discipline. Traditionally, police agencies consider traffic enforcement a less important responsibility than crime prevention and apprehension. Police officials have shown a willingness to participate in planning for enforcement of bus priority projects, yet, quite naturally, they have hesitated to make an extensive commitment of manpower for a continuing enforcement program.

Often the objectives of police officials in enforcement differ from those of the traffic engineer and transportation planner, being oriented toward safety rather than the movement of traffic. Police officials have listed the objectives of traffic law enforcement as follows (*5*):

1. Avoidance of dangerous driver behavior,
2. Removal of impaired drivers from the highway system,

3. Education of drivers, and
4. Inducement of voluntary compliance.

Conspicuous in its absence is the objective of moving traffic more efficiently. Police agencies place emphasis on voluntary compliance and have recognized that traffic enforcement cannot overcome design deficiencies that encourage noncompliance. However, police attitudes that place little importance on efficient traffic flow lead to less enthusiastic and effective enforcement of bus priority measures.

Traffic Engineers

Traffic engineers generally have established a close working relationship with police agencies on traditional traffic control measures. In addition, traffic engineers have worked with transit operators in integrating bus and vehicular operations. As a result, the traffic engineer could provide the most comprehensive approach to bus priority treatment and is in a position to coordinate enforcement, planning, design, and operation. However, more emphasis appears to have been placed on automobile traffic flow; and coordinated design and implementation of bus priority measures, including enforcement, has often been neglected by the professional who could provide the leadership.

Transportation Planners

Emphasis on TSM has redirected the attention of transportation planners from long-range to short-range planning and increasingly has involved planners in operational planning for all modes. In most cases these planners have had little training in traffic enforcement and are limited in their understanding of police attitudes toward enforcement. As a result, enforcement is rarely considered during the planning process. Projects are developed, programmed, and implemented without proper coordination to ensure that enforcement considerations are incorporated at the design stage.

Transit Operators

Enforcement has been pinpointed by transit operators as being a critical factor in the success or failure of bus priority treatments. So critical is enforcement believed to be to the successful operation of bus lanes on CBD arterials that transit officials have sought and secured enforcement authority to remove illegal vehicles from the bus lane (*6*). Although transit operators have intense motivation for enforcement, they often lack experience in identifying enforcement requirements and developing enforcement plans in advance of implementing a bus priority project. Thus they are dependent on the traffic engineer and the police agency for proper identification of enforcement requirements and development of plans.

In many cases, the transit operator is a regional public entity or a private operator that is not a unit of local government. This intensifies the difficulty of coordination among transit, traffic engineering, and law enforcement officials.

Special Interest Groups

Individuals or groups that are affected by bus priority treatment often attempt to influence or modify policy decisions and enforcement regulations on a particular project. These special interest groups can include abutting property owners, taxi operators, delivery services, common carriers, neighborhood organizations, etc., all of which are affected by bus priority restrictions, particularly those on urban arterial facilities. These groups generally feel that they are penalized either financially or esthetically, or that they are inconvenienced by travel restrictions due to bus priority treatment. An educational process is often required in advance of the project to emphasize the general benefits to be achieved by bus priority treatment.

General Public

The general public can be expected to develop an attitude of opposition to sudden, inconvenient changes in traffic flow. Such an attitude, if not offset by educational programs or good geometric design, may result in noncompliance with traffic regulations to an extent that enforcement is difficult or impossible and respect for traffic regulations in general is reduced. Public response and driver reaction to the bus priority project must be considered early in the design phase and can be modified with education programs.

OBJECTIVES OF ENFORCEMENT

The diverse actions, attitudes, procedures, and objectives of the agencies, special interest groups, and the general public in bus priority treatment require close coordination in the design of the project. Lack of coordination will result in confusion in the objectives for the project and make enforcement difficult.

Two primary objectives of traffic enforcement can be identified:

- To reduce accident conditions and improve safety in traffic operations.
- To maintain or improve traffic flow through regulation of driver behavior.

Of these two objectives, the first has received primary attention because of the importance placed upon it by police officials and by the public in general. Repeated traffic accidents at a single location brings a concentrated enforcement response and possible geometric modifications, almost irrespective of cost. The second objective, which is of primary concern in bus priority enforcement, demands cost effectiveness and recognizes that both overenforcement and improper enforcement can cause a deterioration in traffic flow. Under this objective, continuous evaluation of the improvement in traffic flow in relation to the cost of additional enforcement must be conducted.

The specific objectives of the enforcement of bus priority operations recognize the importance of the success or failure of the project itself. These objectives are:

- To enhance the movement of transit vehicles.
- To maintain the integrity of the bus priority project.
- To maintain a tolerable violation rate.

The most common cause of failure of bus priority projects has been the cost of enforcement to maintain the integrity of the project. Frequently, when public officials feel that the cost of enforcement is unreasonable (or when the enforcement sufficient to maintain the project's integrity results in a deterioration in traffic flow), the project is scrapped.

A tolerable violation rate has been applied primarily to preferential bus (and HOV) lanes on freeways. The violation rate is defined as the number of illegal users of the facility expressed as a percentage of the total users of the facility. Generally, a tolerable violation rate is the number of violations that could occur without reducing the travel time advantage for legal HOV using the lane. These rates have been as high as 25 percent on some freeway HOV projects (*7–11*).

However, bus priority treatment on urban streets requires more rigid enforcement. For example, a single violation, such as an illegally parked vehicle on a CBD bus lane, can jeopardize the total effectiveness of the project. The objectives for enforcement of arterial bus priority treatment may establish a tolerable violation rate with respect to following critical violations: (a) parking in a bus lane, (b) stopping or standing in a bus lane, (c) illegal left or right turn across a bus lane, and (d) illegal pedestrian movements (*3*).

The measures of the effectiveness of bus priority enforcement include:

- Number of observed violations.
- Number of critical violations.
- Percentage of time the bus lane is interrupted, including interruptions for use of a towing vehicle to remove violators.

These three measures of effectiveness are each related to a tolerable violation rate or an acceptable threshold; however, the second is unique in that one critical violation is intolerable. Tolerable violation rates should be considered for each bus priority project. The enforcement program of each project should be monitored to determine the violation rate and its relationship to the tolerable rate.

APPROACH TO ENFORCEMENT OF BUS PRIORITY TREATMENT

The approach to enforcement of bus priority treatment on urban streets involves: (a) planning for the facility that includes coordination of all participating agencies; (b) proper design to facilitate enforcement; (c) public education programs; (d) cost-effective enforcement techniques; and (e) improved adjudication procedures. Specifically, the following steps (which are discussed in detail in subsequent chapters) must be taken to ensure successful enforcement:

1. Development of an enforcement plan for bus priority projects,
2. Consideration of project design in relation to enforcement requirements,
3. Development of a program for public education on the project operation,
4. Application of cost-effective enforcement techniques, and
5. Development of improved adjudication procedures.

REFERENCES

1. LEVINSON, H. S., C. L. ADAMS, and W. F. HOEY. *NCHRP Report 155: Bus Use of Highways: Planning and Design Guidelines*. Transportation Research Board, Washington, D.C. (1975) 161 pp.
2. Public Technology, Inc. *Manual on Planning and Implementing Priority Techniques for High-Occupancy Vehicles: Technical Guide*. U.S. Department of Transportation, Washington, D.C. (1977)
3. MILLER, N. C., and R. B. DEUSER. *Enforcement Requirements for High-Occupancy Vehicle Facilities*. Report No. FHWA-RD-79-15. Federal Highway Administration, Washington, D.C. (1978)
4. MEYER, M. D., J. SHELDON-DEAN, and Y. SVORAI. *Enforcement as a Consideration in TSM Planning: A Review of Current Practice*. Center for Transportation Studies, Massachusetts Institute of Technology (1979)
5. SLAVIN, J. M. Traffic Supervision. P. 191 in *Local Government Police Management*. International City Management Association, Washington, D.C. (1977)
6. ERIKSON, G., W. E. HURRELL, and B. W. NELSON. Transit Lane Enforcement in the Central City. Pp. 75–82 in *Transportation Research Record 816: Transportation System Management—Parking, Enforcement, and Other Issues*. Transportation Research Board, Washington, D.C. (1981)
7. Oregon Department of Transportation. *Banfield High Occupancy Vehicle Lanes*. Report No. FHWA-RD-78-59. Federal Highway Administration, Washington D.C. (1978)
8. Oregon Department of Transportation. *Evaluation of Incentives for Carpooling and Bus Use, Banfield Freeway*. Report No. FHWA-RD-78-207. Federal Highway Administration, Washington, D.C. (1978)
9. Bothman, R. N. Banfield Freeway High Occupancy Vehicle Lanes. *Preferential Facilities for Carpools and Buses—Seven Reports*, U.S. Department of Transportation, Washington, D.C. (1976)
10. Oregon Department of Transportation. Banfield Freeway—Analysis of 3-Person to 2-Person HOV Lane Use. Unpublished paper by Transportation Analysis Unit, Metro Branch, Oregon DOT (1978)
11. Oregon Department of Transportation. Banfield Freeway HOV Statistics Report. Unpublished report for the Technical Advisory Committee (1981)

CHAPTER THREE

THE ENFORCEMENT PLAN

To achieve its objectives, a bus priority project must be coordinated among the various departments and disciplines that will design, implement, operate, and enforce the bus priority measure. This includes the participants previously identified in Chapter 2 as well as the public users of the roadway and adjacent facilities. Coordination of all functional aspects as well as identification of the means for successfully operating and enforcing the project can best be achieved through the development of an enforcement plan.

The enforcement plan documents decisions by and agreements among the participating agencies of the project team for a bus priority measure. Early involvement of all parties in the design of a bus priority project and in the development of an enforcement plan permits all aspects of the project and all perspectives of the participants to be considered. Since most bus priority strategies involve operational changes for both the transit system and the driving public, reactions must be anticipated and strategies delineated to minimize negative impacts. An enforcement plan identifies the necessary actions of the project team members and assigns responsibility for their accomplishment. The plan is a necessary supplement to project design, relating project operation to required enforcement as a major design consideration.

REASONS FOR AN ENFORCEMENT PLAN

The following reasons for developing an enforcement plan have been suggested (*1*, p. 79):

- Field officers responsible for day-to-day enforcement are often not the same officers who are directly involved in the planning effort.
- A well-documented, comprehensive enforcement plan may assist in the defense of the project against legal challenges.
- The enforcement plan provides project operating personnel with information on the actions of enforcement officers.
- The activity of developing the plan may in itself highlight previously unanticipated problems, which can then be resolved by the project team before project implementation.

CONTENT OF PLAN

The enforcement plan should contain a description of the project and its objectives, operational procedures, enforcement activities, specific responsibilities, and contingency actions. If properly developed, the plan becomes an excellent reference document and standard operating procedure for use by the transit operator and the enforcing agency in a bus priority project. A manual developed by Public Technology, Inc., for the U.S. Department of Transportation recommends the following outline for the enforcement plan (*1*, p. 83):

ENFORCEMENT PLAN OUTLINE

I. Description of Project
   - A. Objectives and Purpose
   - B. Physical Features

II. System Operations
   - A. Operating Policies
   - B. Operating Hours
   - C. Personnel Level

III. Enforcement Procedures
   - A. Routine Enforcement
   - B. Procedures for Possible Malfunctions
   - C. Emergency Situation Guide
   - D. Reporting Procedures
   - E. Special Intersection Considerations

IV. References

COORDINATION MECHANISM

Preparation of the enforcement plan must be accomplished as a joint effort of all the participants. The continuing need of coordination during the operation of a bus priority measure has often led to the formal establishment of a coordination mechanism in contrast to an ad-hoc structure during project design. The city of San Francisco, for example, maintains a Transit Preferential Streets Coordinating Committee consisting of two planners from the transit operator, a preferential-streets designer from the Public Works Department, a traffic-management planner from the Police Department, and a preferential-transit projects coordinator from the City Planning Department. This committee operates as a staff-level interagency group and provides a monitoring effort for operation and enforcement of bus priority projects as well as a focal point for creative development of additional bus priority strategies.

EDUCATIONAL EFFORTS

The enforcement plan must also include an education program for participants who normally cannot be represented directly by the coordination mechanism. This includes the owners of property and operations adjacent to the bus priority project, the public users of the street and sidewalk facilities, and the municipal court judges who will be called upon to adjudicate enforcement citations. The plan must include specific means by which the general public and the judiciary can gain an understanding of and respect for the operation of the bus priority measure.

SCOPE OF PLAN

An enforcement plan should be developed for each specific bus priority project in contrast to a general enforcement plan for bus priority treatment in an urban area. Furthermore, a separate enforcement plan should be developed for each increment of a bus priority project that is implemented in segments. The basic concept is an enforcement plan that addresses the design and operational issues of each project segment as it is opened to the public and provides a total program of enforcement for the project.

REFERENCE

1. Public Technology, Inc. *Manual on Planning and Implementing Priority Techniques for High Occupancy Vehicles: Technical Guide.* U.S. Department of Transportation, Washington, D.C. (1977)

CHAPTER FOUR

A TOTAL PROGRAM OF ENFORCEMENT

A total program of enforcement is necessary in bus priority treatment to achieve an acceptable violation rate and to maintain project integrity. Traditional and nontraditional enforcement techniques must be combined with promotional efforts to gain public support. A total program of enforcement should include the following elements:

- Public education
- Informational programs for traffic court judges
- Traditional enforcement techniques
- Nontraditional enforcement techniques
- Combined enforcement techniques
- Establishment of adequate penalties for violators
- Legal responsibilities and adjudication procedures

VIOLATIONS

It should be stressed that the most significant enforcement problems in bus priority treatment have been (a) parked or waiting cars and double parking by delivery vehicles in dense retail areas and (b) the identification and apprehension of ineligible users when car-pools are permitted to use an HOV lane. Enforcement of bus-only priority treatment in the form of exclusive lanes has proven to be more successful because of (a) limited access points for buses only and (b) the fact that violators in a bus-only lane are more conspicuous than in an HOV lane (and thus the propensity toward such violations is reduced).

It should also be noted that two types of traffic law violators have been identified: (a) the willful violator who knowingly risks apprehension and fines to gain the travel-time advantage in an HOV lane: and (b) the nondeliberate violator who is confused by the unusual traffic flows associated with bus priority treatment. The enforcement program must be developed to apprehend both types of violators.

PUBLIC EDUCATION

Public education is extremely important in any new bus priority treatment and enforcement program. The more complex the bus priority project and the more significant the traffic changes, the more important public education becomes. As the public better understands the objectives of the bus priority treatment and the enforcement necessary to make the system work, the better its response will be to voluntary compliance and to the project itself.

Identification of special interest groups within the general public is necessary to target public information efforts. In dense retail areas, for example, where curbside deliveries are the rule, special efforts should be made to inform the abutting merchants, delivery services, and labor organizations on the objective of the bus priority project and the restrictions associated with its operation.

In San Francisco, where there is an aggressive program of bus priority treatment in the core area, the transit preferential streets coordinator makes personal contact with abutting property owners before project implementation to discuss utilization of curb space and design of the priority bus lane. Immediately before initiating the bus priority operation, a letter is sent to abutting property owners reiterating the project objectives and offering assistance during initial operation.

For the Madison Avenue dual-width bus-lane project in New York City, various handbills were developed for distribution to motorists, bus riders, and pedestrians, with each handbill providing the specific information needed by each group (Figure 3). Special handbills were also distributed to taxi operators to explain changes in taxi regulations necessitated by the opening of the bus lane (Figure 4).

The following items should be addressed in a public education program:

- Objectives of the bus priority project and how the project will fit into the overall transportation plan,
- Location and operating hours of the project,
- Anticipated beneficiaries of the project (e.g., buses, taxis),
- Use of the project and benefits for the traveling public,
- New traffic regulations or restrictions, and
- Person to contact for more information.

With respect to enforcement, the public should be provided with information on (*1*, p. 7):

- Laws and prohibitions relating to the bus priority project,
- Procedures when violations occur, and
- Consequences of being apprehended or cited for a violation.

The public information program for the opening of a bus priority project must be conducted sufficiently in advance of the project to permit public digestion and response. In addition, if conducted properly, the information program in regard to enforcement can serve as an excellent marketing effort for public transportation. Repeated information notices can convey that "things are happening in public transportation" and that local and state governments are committed to enforcement measures for improved traffic flows.

It is suggested that a public education program include the following stages:

- Advance notices of the proposed project including a description of anticipated results. These notices should be provided beginning 3 to 4 months in advance of the project.
- Intense effort of information releases during the initial weeks of bus priority operation.

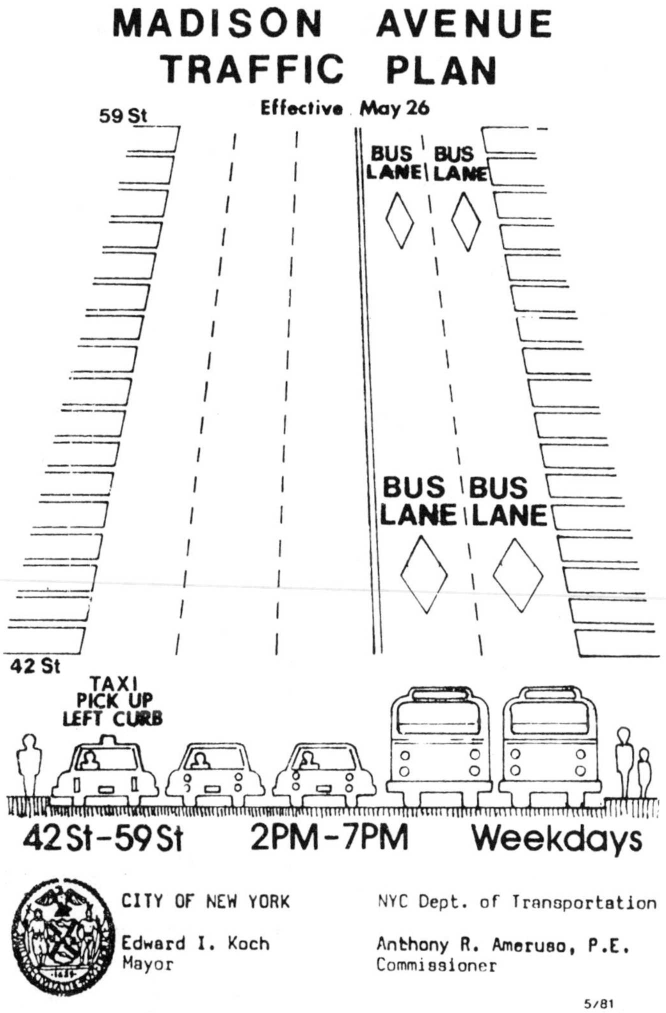

MADISON AVENUE DUAL BUS LANE

Beginning May 26, 1981, 2PM to 7PM
Monday through Friday. *

Right two lanes buses only.

Traffic in left three lanes free from competition with buses.

Authorized parking (diplomats, press, etc.) removed.

Right turns prohibited from 44 to 59 Streets inclusive.

People will find cabs only on the left (west) side of the Avenue.

Taxis with passengers allowed to use the bus lane from 42 St. to turn at 44 or 46 Street. (No pick-ups or discharges permitted in bus lanes.)

The Benefits:

Commuters, shoppers, tourists can be sure of a 10 minute bus ride from 42 to 59 Streets. (Now 15 to 30 minutes.)

Service will improve for 24,000 riders. (2/3 of all people using Madison Avenue travel in buses.)

Smoother and faster traffic flow will reduce air pollution.

Madison Avenue will be a better environment for pedestrians.

*NOTE: At other hours and on weekends, the bus lanes will not be in effect. Cars, taxis and trucks may travel in all lanes.

FIGURE 3 Example of handbill distributed to motorists, bus riders, and pedestrians to provide information on the Madison Avenue (New York City) dual-width bus-lane project *(front and back of flyer are shown)*. (New York City DOT.)

• Dissemination of the results of the bus priority project in an effort to describe the success of the project and delineate enforcement activities.

• Continuing public education through the news media as well as informational programs for special interest groups and neighborhood meetings, depending on the extent of the bus priority project. Commercially printed pamphlets and professionally developed television advertisements may be appropriate.

INFORMATIONAL PROGRAMS FOR TRAFFIC COURT JUDGES

A major limitation in the enforcement of bus priority treatment has been the hesitancy of traffic judges to process citations issued for bus-lane violations. As the judiciary has a major role in enforcement, ignorance or lack of support on the part of traffic court judges can weaken enforcement programs. Before implementation of bus priority projects, local traffic judges should be informed of the project objectives, the revised traffic restrictions, and the enforcement procedures to be used. Special presentations to judges to promote a fuller appreciation of a project is desirable. Judges should be encouraged to investigate previous court rulings on enforcement citations.

TRADITIONAL ENFORCEMENT TECHNIQUES

Traditional traffic law enforcement techniques that have been used effectively in bus priority treatment are discussed below.

Officer Education

Although not specifically an enforcement technique, a special program for the education and orientation of police officers on enforcement of bus priority treatment is beneficial. The purpose of enforcement and its importance to efficient traffic flow should be stressed. Often, police officers, lacking an understanding of the purpose of enforcement, apprehend violators in the bus lane, thereby contributing to the problem of lane blockage (see Figure 5).

Use of Civilian Enforcement Officers

Although this technique is primarily limited to a core CBD area, special civilian officers can provide an enforcement arm dedicated to achieving traffic objectives. This can dispel

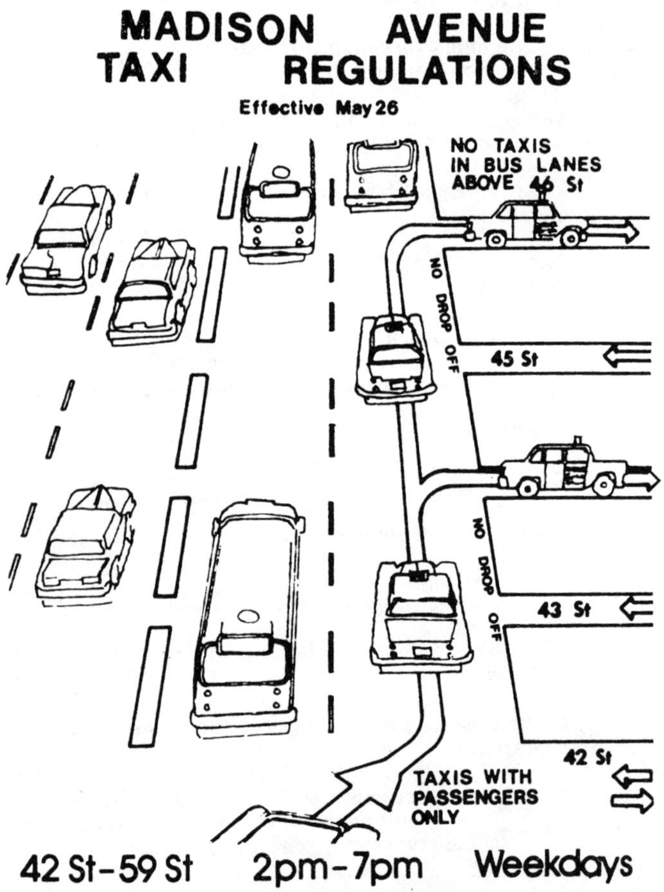

MADISON AVENUE DUAL BUS LANE
(42-59 St.)

Beginning May 26, 1981, 2PM to 7PM, Monday through Friday:*

o Right two lanes buses only except that:

Medallion Taxis with passengers may enter the bus lanes only at 42nd Street to turn right at 44th or 46th Street. (NO pick-ups or discharges permitted in bus lane).

o No taxis above 46th Street in bus lane.

o NO right turns will be permitted from mixed traffic lanes 42nd - 59th Streets (except for taxis in the bus lane, see above).

o All pick-ups and discharges from the west curb only.

o Traffic in left three lanes free from competition with buses.

*NOTE: At other hours and on weekends, the bus lanes will not be in effect. Cars, taxis, and trucks may travel in all lanes.

FIGURE 4 Example of handbill distributed to taxi operators explaining new taxi regulations required by implementation of the Madison Avenue (New York City) dual-width bus-lane project *(front and back of flyer are shown)*. (New York City DOT.)

FIGURE 5 Enforcement procedures block transit lane in San Francisco (*7*).

the negative public relations aspect of apprehension by an armed policeman. Civilian officers who are assigned daily to a specific beat establish a close working relationship with transit operators and abutting property owners and often can provide a continuing and positive informational effort for the bus priority project.

Official Warning

This technique is primarily used to advise ineligible users of HOV or bus-only lanes that their illegal use of the lane has been observed. An official warning in standard letter format is sent to violators who are observed or who are identified by means of photographs. The owner of the vehicle is assumed to be the violator. Miller and Deuser (*1*, p. 7) reported driver response to the official warning to be good in an evaluation of the San Francisco-Oakland Bay Bridge priority lane project.

Off-Street Apprehension of Violators

Apprehension of violators in exclusive bus lanes is difficult if no refuge areas (areas outside the moving traffic stream, e.g., cross streets, alleys, special-purpose bays) are available. Various nontraditional methods are often used if refuge areas are not accessible.

Deterrent Fines

Fines must be sufficiently expensive to discourage violators. As the use of the exclusive lane by willful violators is primarily for the purpose of saving time, it is beneficial to the violator to risk apprehension if the penalty is in the form of a low-cost fine. A special effort is needed to maintain fines in a cost range high enough to make the risk prohibitive to willful violators. Fines ranging as high as $50 per violation have been used in Philadelphia to discourage bus-lane violations. Also, considering bus-lane violations as moving violations adds to the severity of offense and discourages repeat offenders.

Posting of Fines

When deterrent fines are used to discourage bus-lane violations, posting of the fine amount can increase public awareness and compliance. The amount of the fine can be posted on signs delineating the bus lane and specifying the traffic restrictions: e.g., "Limited to buses between 7:00–9:00 a.m. and 4:00–6:00 p.m. $50 fine for unauthorized use of bus lane."

Visible Enforcement

Police officials often maintain that the visibility of the enforcement official in traffic operations is more effective than actual enforcement. In enforcement of exclusive bus lanes (particularly on high-speed arterials), however, visible enforcement can result in safety hazards caused by violators who suddenly exit the exclusive lane when they observe a police officer.

Initial Enforcement Saturation

Heavy enforcement during the initial operations of the bus priority treatment has been effective in public orientation and in discouraging willful violators. In the Madison Avenue dual-width bus-lane project in New York City, normal enforcement was tripled during implementation phases. Professional traffic personnel with two-way radio communication closely monitored each block. A radio control center and elevated command post provided overall control and permitted immediate response to disruptions.

Consistent Enforcement

Most bus priority measures require a consistent level of enforcement for successful operation. Enforcement officials in Seattle and Minneapolis report that violations increased substantially following reduced enforcement due to manpower shortages, inclement weather, etc. Experimentation can provide the minimum level of consistent enforcement necessary to maintain the level of service desired for the bus priority operations.

Mobile and On-Foot Enforcement

Even though most traffic enforcement traditionally is accomplished by police officers in patrol cars, effective enforcement on bus priority projects can be achieved by on-foot patrols. This is true not only for curb-lane enforcement but also for median-lane enforcement where refuge areas are available to on-foot patrolmen for apprehending violators. Scooter-mounted patrols have been used effectively in Washington, D.C., for bus priority and parking enforcement.

NONTRADITIONAL ENFORCEMENT TECHNIQUES

Nontraditional techniques that are available for bus priority enforcement are described below.

Team Concept—Remote Apprehension

On median-lane bus priority projects without refuge areas, apprehension of violators is difficult because of the necessity to manuever both patrol car and violator to the outside lane. By working in teams with radio communication, enforcement officers can identify violators and then apprehend them at a convenient and safe location.

Photographic Identification of Violators

Courts have recognized that photographs may be relevant to enforcement and may be introduced as evidence to establish identities. Objections and legal questions have been raised, however, in regard to invasion of privacy. Camera equipment is currently available for use in bus priority enforcement, and the Federal Highway Administration has conducted research on the use of photography to record vehicle occupancy.

Mailed Citations

Photographic identification of violators leads to mailed citations. Citations may also be mailed in response to observed violations as was the case in enforcement operations for the Southeast Expressway (Boston) concurrent-flow HOV lane.

License-Plate Analysis for Repeat Violators

A technique for the mass screening of license plates has been explored recently by the Maryland Motor Vehicle Administration, the Maryland State Police, and the Insurance Institute for Highway Safety (*1*, p. 169). The system permits the rapid screening of a license-plate number to identify and detain habitual violators at apprehension. This system may also be used for mailing and other means of issuing citations.

Travel-Time Penalty

An effective means of enforcement is making the violator, through traffic control devices or manual direction, take a more circuitous route than he normally would take. This can be enforced for median-lane bus priority by on-foot patrolmen; however, this method is more effective in freeway travel than on urban streets. On I-93 in Boston, an additional travel time of 20 min for violators resulted from this means of enforcement. The travel-time penalty has been well received by both law enforcement officials and motorists because: (a) the penalty is appropriate for the violation; (b) traffic is not disrupted; (c) enforcement procedures apprehend almost all violators; (d) no special equipment or refuge area is required; and (e) the officer's time is not consumed by court appearances (*1*, p. 33).

Transit Service Checkers as Enforcement Officers

Authorizing transit service checkers or inspectors to issue citations for both moving and parking violations in the exclusive transit lane offers a way to provide additional enforcement for bus priority treatment, particularly in dense central areas. San Francisco is the only city thus far to implement such a program, and it has been judged moderately successful by both police and transit officials. Inspectors are stationed on foot at major intersections and have the authority to flag down and cite motorists for moving violations. Due to the pace of transit operations during the peak hours, inspectors in San Francisco have been instructed to cite violators only in off-peak hours (*2*, p. 24).

Parked, Unoccupied Patrol Car

The procedure of stationing an empty patrol car in a visible location where violations have been high has been used in Sacramento, California. This has been reported to be especially effective in enforcing moving violations and can be combined with on-foot enforcement in dense areas. The difficulty in finding an appropriate location to park the vacant patrol car in a CBD core area has made the practice questionable for dense areas. The unavailability of patrol cars for this purpose has also proven to be a major disadvantage (*2*, p. 29).

Towing of Illegally Parked Vehicles

An effective means of enforcing parking restrictions on exclusive bus lanes has been a towing and impounding program. This program is particularly applicable to bus priority enforcement in that it provides a means of quickly removing a critical violation as well as a costly punitive action in terms of both time and money. Such a program has been used in Washington, D.C., since 1978 as an effective means of parking enforcement. Privately owned towing services, responding within minutes to the summons of a patrol officer, can quickly remove critical violations without lengthy disruptions of the exclusive bus lane (*3–5*).

COMBINED ENFORCEMENT TECHNIQUES

The most cost-effective enforcement efforts often combine several different techniques. For example, the combination of mailed citations and increased fines with the travel-time penalty can reduce enforcement costs without decreasing effectiveness.

LEGAL RESPONSIBILITIES AND ADJUDICATION PROCEDURES

Most courts have found that state and local governments have the power to initiate bus priority projects and that enforcement of bus priority treatment is within the police powers of the governmental agencies. A legal opinion should be sought before implementing a bus priority project if previous decisions have not clearly defined the entity's legal responsibilities.

Adjudication procedures should be established to permit fines to be paid by mail and with as little inconvenience as possible to the public. Preventive measures should lie in the amount of the fine, not in the inconvenience of paying the fine. In Washington, D.C., an adjudication procedure for parking violations has been implemented whereby the proceedings have been moved from a criminal court to an adjudication environment in which hearings are conducted informally. The usual criminal-court delays are avoided, and vigorous follow-up procedures on violators through repeated notification, vehicle-registration deferral, and an integrated data system have improved enforcement (*6*).

REFERENCES

1. Miller, N. C. and R. B. Deuser. *Enforcement Requirements for High-Occupancy Vehicle Facilities*. Report No. FHWA-RD-79-15. Federal Highway Administration, Washington, D.C. (1978)
2. Wilbur Smith & Associates. *Non-Traditional Enforcement Techniques—Transit Preferential Streets Program*. Urban Mass Transportation Administration, U.S. Department of Transportation, Washington, D.C. (1980)
3. Brophy, J. M., and H. W. Voccola. Parking Enforcement and Follow Up. Paper presented at 25th Annual IMPC Conference, Hollywood, Florida, April 10, 1979.
4. DiRenzo, J. F., et al. *Study of Parking Management Tactics*. Volume 2. *Overview and Case Studies*. Report No. FHWA-PL-79-021. U.S. Department of Transportation, Washington, D.C. (1979)
5. Brophy, J. Criteria for a Balanced Parking Program. Paper presented at the 23rd Annual Parking Workshop, Institutional and Municipal Parking Congress, June 8, 1977.
6. Transportation Research Board. *NCHRP Synthesis 81: Experiences in Transportation System Management*. Washington, D.C. (1981) 88 pp.
7. Erickson, G., W. E. Hurrell, and B. W. Nelson. Transit Lane Enforcement in the Central City. Pp. 75–82 in *Transportation Research Record 816: Transportation System Management—Parking, Enforcement, and Other Issues*. Transportation Research Board, Washington, D.C. (1981)

CHAPTER FIVE

ENFORCEMENT AND PROJECT DESIGN BY TYPE OF PRIORITY TREATMENT

Priority treatment for buses on urban streets generally involves the use of buses on arterial facilities that have limited access from abutting property and that permit, under off-peak conditions, turning movements (right and left, onto and off the facility). Project design must consider the possible conflicts between bus priority and other functions of the arterial: e.g., property access, vehicular traffic flow, on-street parking, etc. Enforcement becomes a major consideration when other roadway functions are restricted in favor of the bus. Project design must recognize the importance as well as the expense of enforcement, and features must be incorporated in the design that will encourage self enforcement of vehicle and pedestrian restrictions, while maintaining traditional design considerations, such as visibility, uniformity, and motorist understanding.

Successful bus priority operations on arterial streets have involved the dedication of exclusive bus lanes and the use of signal-emitting equipment for bus priority through traffic signals, either isolated or system controlled. Also, entire roadways have been successfully reserved for buses as have automobile-restricted zones, principally in core areas. The following factors should be considered in evaluating alternatives for bus priority treatment and in designing projects:

- Street widths and facility capacity
- Number of traffic lanes
- Traffic volumes and speeds
- Anticipated changes in traffic flow as a result of project restrictions
- Cross streets and cross-traffic volumes
- Turning movements
- Median type and width
- Vehicle travel times and delays (including buses)
- Curb-parking controls
- Bus passenger loading (curb or off-street)
- Abutting land use and property access and future growth
- Traffic generation by abutting property
- Adjacent major parking facilities
- Bus routing and volume
- Conflicts with pedestrian traffic

It should be noted that many of the above factors can be modified or restricted to facilitate bus priority (e.g., number of traffic lanes, curb parking, turning movements); however, such restrictions must be enforced. Thus enforcement must be considered early in the project design phase.

General guidelines for enforcement and design and specific design guidelines for four types of bus priority measures, as well as the violations that can be expected on each type of bus priority treatment and effective enforcement measures, are discussed in this chapter. The four general types of bus priority measures are:

1. Concurrent-Flow Bus Lanes
2. Contraflow Bus Lanes
3. Bus-Only Streets and Automobile-Restricted Zones
4. Signal Preemption

GENERAL GUIDELINES FOR ENFORCEMENT AND DESIGN

Excellent general design guidelines for bus priority treatment on urban streets are presented in *NCHRP Report 155: Bus Use of Highways: Planning and Design Guidelines* (*1*). Guidelines specifically related to enforcement and design are presented below, and specific design features that support enforcement are identified under each type of bus priority measure. General design guidelines for more efficient enforcement strategies include:

- Bus priority projects should be designed in conformance with AASHTO (*2*) and MUTCD (*3*) standards to the greatest extent possible.
- Bus priority treatment should provide improved service (reduced travel time and improved schedule adherence) to a significant number of bus routes. Enforcement of infrequently used bus priority facilities is difficult.
- Any traffic restrictions imposed as a result of bus priority treatment for the purpose of travel-time savings should be in effect only during those time periods when the travel-time savings can be achieved.
- Bus priority treatment, particularly in dense core areas, must consider competing uses of curb space. The design must take into consideration alternative means of service deliveries, curb pickup, entrances to parking facilities, etc.
- A bus priority project should be designed for initial operation over its entire length (at least in one direction). Staged construction and incremental openings result in significant enforcement problems.

CONCURRENT-FLOW BUS LANES

The concurrent-flow bus lane is the most commonly used bus priority treatment on urban streets, and generally involves the reservation of either the curb lane or median lane for the operation of buses in the same direction as other vehicular traffic on an arterial. The objective of concurrent-flow priority treatment is to provide buses with a travel-time advantage over congested traffic in other lanes.

The choice of the lane to be used exclusively for buses should only be made after an evaluation of the existing geometric design of the roadway, the type of transit service provided, land uses abutting the arterial facility, and the current use of the curb lane, either for parking or for delivery vehicles. In general, median lanes are used for line-haul bus routes on urban arterials where bus stops are infrequent or nonexistent; curb lanes are used when passenger service dictates frequent bus stops. The use of interior lanes for bus priority treatment may be necessary in dense core areas where curb space is particularly critical. Heavy use of the curb lane by delivery vehicles, particularly where no other means of goods delivery is possible, may dictate the use of interior lanes.

Concurrent-flow bus lanes have been implemented in major cities in the United States and throughout Europe and Canada. They have been used extensively in London, where more than 150 individual, discontinuous bus lanes, covering a total of 26 miles, are in use, with additional lanes planned. Bus lanes are provided where more than 35 buses per hour use a given arterial roadway. Enforcement of the parking ban on bus lanes is strict; traffic wardens are equipped with nearly universal keys and simply drive away the offending cars (*4*, p. 47).

As the type of bus service on urban streets (i.e., line haul or frequent passenger pickup and discharge) is generally different on median bus lanes compared to curbside lanes, these two approaches to concurrent-flow bus priority treatment are discussed separately.

Median Lane on Arterial Roadway

Under this approach, the median lane of an urban arterial is restricted for use by buses and, in most cases, by HOV. (The definition of HOV varies by application. Perhaps the most common definition includes all vehicles with two or more occupants, although many projects restrict use of the lane to vehicles with three or more occupants.) First priority is given to buses, and use of the lane by HOV is restricted when heavy HOV use leads to a reduced level of service for buses. Operation of the HOV lane is generally limited to morning and evening peak periods. Buses operate nonstop on the facility.

Design features for bus priority treatment involving the use of a concurrent-flow median lane are given in Table 1. Two significant factors should be stressed. First, enforcement of the exclusive lane is difficult when limited use is made of the lane by buses or HOV. Sixty to ninety buses per hour is considered as the minimum for bus flow on the exclusive lane to achieve public acceptance and reasonable voluntary compliance. Second, at least two traffic lanes should be available for other vehicular traffic in the same direction as the exclusive lane. Excessive delay to other vehicular traffic as a result of inadequate lane capacity can be expected to result in willful violations of the exclusive bus lane.

South Dixie Highway (Florida) Project

A median lane on the South Dixie Highway (U.S. Route 1) in Florida was dedicated for exclusive concurrent flow of buses and HOV in April 1976. A project of the Florida Department of Transportation and Metropolitan Dade County, the exclusive lane is operated from 6:00 to 9:00 a.m. and from 4:00 to 7:00 p.m. over a 5.5-mile segment from Sunset Drive to the Miami CBD. Based on an extensive evaluation effort after 2 years of operation, bus ridership had increased fivefold during that period and transit travel times had been reduced significantly. In buses and HOV combined, the exclusive lane carries 40 percent of the persons using the six-lane arterial during the peak hour.

Modifications in traffic flow were necessary to support the exclusive lane. Signs were placed to identify the separate lane for buses and carpools. Roadway striping is used at all median openings to prohibit left turns through the bus lane. Left turns onto the arterial facility are permitted. Signal modifications include improved progression, extended cycle length, and reduction to two phases, with left turns from the arterial prohibited during operation of the exclusive lane.

Enforcement measures played an important role in the selection of the concurrent-flow median-lane operation. The project was initially operated as a contraflow lane for approximately 21 months but was changed to concurrent-flow operation primarily as a result of high costs for enforcement of the contraflow operation and for manual placement of traffic cones to delineate the exclusive lane. In its current form, the project illustrates successful operation of an arterial concurrent-flow median-lane bus priority measure.

Types of Violations

Operational experience with median-lane priority treatment has identified two types of violations:

Unauthorized Use of Exclusive Lane This violation is most prevalent when the exclusive lane is also open to HOV and generally involves vehicles with less than the required number of occupants for a defined carpool. The violation rate can run as high as 75 to 80 percent if restricted use is not enforced. Violations of this type, however, are not critical unless the violation rate is high enough to restrict use by buses and legitimate HOV (this depends on the number of buses and HOV using the exclusive lane). Enforcement of this type of violation is difficult because of (a) the surveillance required to readily identify violators if the lane is open to HOV (violators of bus-only lanes are easily identified); and (b) difficulty in apprehending violators without restricting traffic flow in the exclusive lane or in other traffic lanes. However, lack of enforcement, particularly if bus and HOV traffic is light, will reduce respect for traffic controls in general.

Illegal Left Turns Across Exclusive Lane Most median-lane bus priority projects permit left turns onto the arterial facility but prohibit left turns from the arterial across the exclusive lane. Omitting left-turn phases from signalized intersections provides additional green time to the exclusive lane. Left-turn bays on the arterial are usually striped or signed to

TABLE 1
FEATURES OF CONCURRENT-FLOW BUS LANES

A. Median Lane on Arterial Roadway

Design Features

Lane Width	Design Speed[a]	Minimum One-Way Bus Volume	Practical Minimum Length	Roadway	Refuge Areas
12 ft	45–60 mph	60–90 buses/hr	2 miles (less, if effective in eliminating or reducing bus delay)	At least 2 lanes available for other traffic in same direction	Provide refuge areas in median if sufficient left-turn bays are not available for apprehension of violators

Traffic Control Devices

Signing				
Advance Warning	Restricted Lane	End of Bus Lane	Lane Demarcation	Special Markings
Roadside: R3–10 Overhead: R3–13 (see Figure 6)	Roadside: R3–11 Overhead: R3–14 (see Figure 6)	Roadside: R3–12 Overhead: R3–15 (see Figure 6)	Solid white line for bus-only lanes or 24-hr operation; broken white line for HOV lane and/or peak-hour-only operation	Diamond symbol on bus-lane pavement spaced so as to be in constant view by lane users

Restrictions

1. Hours of operation: During peak period in which bus speeds are increased relative to other vehicular traffic.
2. Turning movements: Prohibition of left turns across the bus lane during hours of priority operation.
3. Use of lane by other vehicles: Public pressure has traditionally required opening bus lane to other HOV, particularly when bus volumes are light and congestion occurs in parallel lanes. Number of passengers required in vehicle classified as HOV can be reduced if it is determined that bus speeds will not be penalized by additional vehicles. Additional enforcement is required if carpools are permitted to use exclusive lane. Taxis are often permitted in CBD bus priority lanes; minimal enforcement problems occur due to recognition potential.

B. Curbside Lane on Arterial Roadway

Design Features

Lane Width	Design Speed[a]	Minimum One-Way Bus Volume	Practical Minimum Length	Roadway	Refuge Areas
11–12 ft (a double lane is often provided in in dense areas to permit buses to pass)	30–45 mph	30–40 buses/hr	2–3 city blocks	At least 2 lanes available for other traffic in same direction	Use cross streets, or special refuge areas if cross streets are not available

Traffic Control Devices

Signing				
Advance Warning	Restricted Lane	End of Bus Lane	Lane Demarcation	Special Markings
Roadside: R3–10 Overhead: R3–13 (see Figure 6)	Roadside: R3–11 Overhead: R3–14 (see Figure 6) (posted in each block as necessary)	Roadside: R3–12 Overhead: R3–15 (see Figure 6)	Solid white line for 24-hr bus operation (use of buttons or other delineators may increase awareness and aid enforcement)	Diamond symbol on bus lane pavement spaced so as to be in constant view by lane users

Restrictions

1. Hours of operation: Continuous or during peak period only. CBD curb lanes are generally operated on 24-hr basis.
2. Turning movements: Right turns are generally permitted (except where bus-lane volumes are heavy), and vehicles are permitted to make right turns from bus lane. Maximum travel distance for right turn in the bus lane should be limited to 1 block.
3. Stopping or standing: Any stopping or standing within bus lane should be prohibited and strictly enforced, as any parked vehicle jeopardizes the function of bus-lane operation.
4. Use of lane by other vehicles: Taxicabs, other vehicles that are loading and unloading passengers, motorcycles, and bicycles may be permitted to travel in curb bus lane if bus-lane volumes are light. Heavy use of curb lane by buses will demand prohibition of all vehicles except for those loading and unloading.

[a] Design speed for geometric design (this is greater than operating speed).

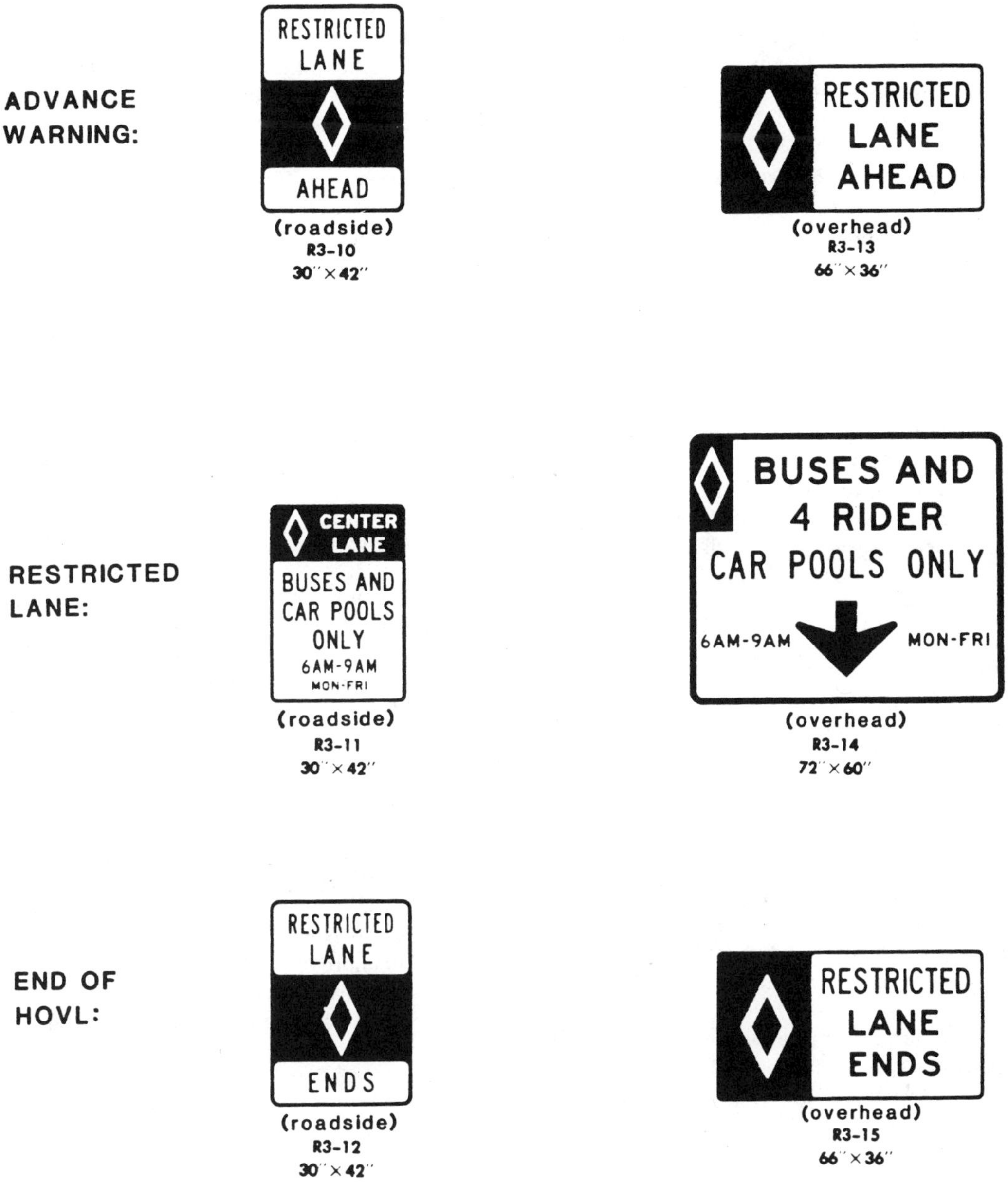

FIGURE 6 Preferential lane-use control signs recommended by MUTCD (*3*).

prohibit their use during hours of operation of the bus or HOV lane. As is the case for violations involving illegal use of the exclusive lane, the left-turn prohibitions are much easier to enforce when the exclusive lane is heavily used. Violations, however, are more critical due to the accident potential of vehicles making left turns across the high-speed exclusive lane.

Effective Enforcement Strategies

In successful median-lane projects, various, and often nonrelated, measures have been combined into effective enforcement strategies.

Public Education and Heavy Initial Enforcement Public education programs describing the purpose and benefits of the project as well as the punitive measures for violations can be effectively combined with heavy initial enforcement of all types of violations. Respect for the project, its success, and its enforcement is thus developed in the initial stages of operation.

Transit Marketing and Good Geometric Design for Bus Access to Exclusive Lane While not strictly an enforcement measure, this combination suggests that "a good offense is more effective than a good defense" as violations are reduced when bus use of exclusive lanes is increased. The

Denver Regional Transportation District reports that violations on its 2-mile exclusive-lane, arterial connection to a major freeway were significantly reduced when bus use approached 80 to 90 buses per hour.

Use of Closed Left-Turn Bays for Both Patrol-Car Observations and Refuge Areas for Apprehending Violators Apprehension of moving violators without median refuge areas requires that violators be maneuvered across other lanes of traffic, thus slowing total traffic flow. Use of closed left-turn bays permits patrolmen on foot and upstream on the median to direct violators to the refuge area.

Team Enforcement for Upstream Identification of Violators Patrolmen working in teams have been effectively used to identify violators upstream and to notify, through radio communications, a patrolman waiting at exits from the exclusive lane. This enforcement measure works well when geometrics restrict egress from the bus or HOV lane.

Curbside Lane on Arterial Roadway

The use of curbside lanes for concurrent-flow bus priority treatment is primarily associated with one-way streets in the CBD or with divided arterials that have sufficient unused capacity. Bus stops for loading and unloading are frequent. Operation of the curb lane exclusively for buses may be accomplished during the peak period or on a 24-hr basis. Use of the exclusive curb lane is generally restricted to buses although taxi use is often permitted, particularly in dense CBD areas. Dual-width lanes are often provided to permit buses to pass during passenger loading and unloading of other buses.

Interior lanes are frequently reserved for buses in dense CBD areas when curb space is limited and must be used for delivery vehicles and parking. The use of both curbside and interior lanes in different sections of a bus priority treatment in a dense area is sometimes mandated by local conditions.

Design features for curbside lanes used for concurrent-flow bus priority treatment are given in Table 1.

Madison Avenue (New York City) Dual-Width Bus-Lane Project

The dual-width curbside bus lane on Madison Avenue in New York City provides an excellent example of concurrent-flow bus lanes in dense urban traffic. Implemented in May 1981, the project operates on Madison Avenue between 42nd and 59th Streets (0.85 miles) from 2:00 to 7:00 p.m. on weekdays. Madison Avenue, a one-way facility, provides a cross section of two 11-ft bus lanes, two 10-ft mixed-traffic lanes, and one 9-ft mixed-traffic curb lane. The project required (a) increasing spacing between bus stops on the curbside bus lane, (b) prohibiting parking on the opposite curb, and (c) prohibiting all right turns. Taxis are permitted to use the bus lanes for a portion of the project due to unusual roadway configurations. Bus volumes average 218 buses per hour during the peak hour and 136 buses per hour during the 5-hr period of operation.

An evaluation of the project reported an average decrease of 40 to 50 percent in bus travel time during the peak hour. Bus ridership was increased and traffic flow in the mixed-traffic lanes improved due to removal of buses from the traffic stream (see Figure 7).

Enforcement efforts for the project included an extensive public-education effort before implementation of the project. Handbills explaining the project's operation were provided to motorists, bus passengers, and taxi drivers. Operation and enforcement were coordinated among transit personnel, traffic engineers, and police officials. Twenty-four civilian enforcement agents were employed and assigned to the 18 intersections within the project during the first year of operation. Consistent enforcement of the project was recognized as an important feature of the project's success.

Transit Preferential Streets Program (San Francisco)

The Transit Preferential Streets Program in San Francisco is an excellent example of the use of concurrent-flow curbside lanes in bus priority treatment in dense urban areas. Bus lanes on Post, Sutter, and Mission Streets in the San Francisco CBD are generally designed as 18-ft lanes at the right curb on one-way streets. Parking and goods delivery are permitted at curbside except during peak hours. A new bus lane on Stockton Street uses an interior lane in blocks where curb use is particularly critical. Right-turning vehicles are permitted to use the restricted lane as are vehicles entering curbside parking spaces. Enforcement has been a major problem, and adequate police involvement has been difficult to achieve. Nevertheless, the San Francisco program has resulted in improved transit schedule adherence and reduced bus travel times. The Stockton Street bus lane, for example, after 5 months of operation, showed a reduction in bus run times and a narrowing of the range of run times (*5*).

Harry Hines Boulevard and Singleton Avenue (Dallas) Curbside Bus Lanes

Two examples of curbside bus lanes on arterial facilities in other than CBD dense areas are the Harry Hines Boulevard and Singleton Avenue projects in Dallas. Both facilities are six-lane divided arterials that are radial to the Dallas CBD. The curbside lane on a 2-mile segment of both roadways is reserved for buses and right-turning vehicles in the peak direction during the peak hours. Bus volumes on Harry Hines Boulevard are 32 buses per hour, and on Singleton, 43 buses per hour. Both roadways serve low-density commercial and industrial land uses. Evaluations of the projects have shown increased speeds on both facilities. Enforcement has presented no problem due to the excess capacity on both roadways (*6*).

Types of Violations

Violations in the operation of curbside bus priority treatment have generally been of three types.

FIGURE 7 Traffic flow on Madison Avenue (New York City) dual-width bus-lane project before (*left*) and after (*right*) implementation of bus priority treatment. (New York City DOT.)

Illegal Parking and Stopping in Bus Lane (Figure 8) This violation involves delivery vehicles, taxicabs, and private automobiles, loading and unloading passengers, and often double-parked tour buses in the larger cities. Each violation is critical since it jeopardizes the priority bus operation; thus effective enforcement must include the immediate removal of the illegal vehicle. The design of the priority bus operation must include an analysis of curb-use demand and provide other alternatives (geographical or temporal) for goods and passenger delivery; otherwise, enforcement of the curbside lane will be difficult or impossible.

Unauthorized Use of Exclusive Lane The use of the curbside bus lane for vehicular right turns is generally permitted. (In New York's Madison Avenue project, right turns are prohibited due to the large volume of buses.) If right turns are permitted, violations can occur when vehicles travel in the bus lane for an excessive distance (generally more than ½ block) before turning right. Violations of this type become critical when bus flow within the lane is affected.

Illegal Pedestrian Maneuvers Heavy pedestrian traffic, particularly across the arterial facility, reduce green signal time for the buses. Illegal pedestrian maneuvers (jaywalking) can necessitate sudden stops by buses, cause bus delays, and create significant safety hazards.

Effective Enforcement Strategies

The importance of enforcement to the successful operation of curbside bus priority strategies is generally recognized. Enforcement measures that have been effectively used for concurrent-flow curbside bus lanes are discussed below.

Use of Civilian Agents or Provision of Police Incentives Civilian agents have been effectively used to enforce curbside bus lanes, particularly in dense areas. The primary function of these special agents, usually on foot or on scooters, is that of traffic enforcement in conjunction with bus priority treatment; traffic flow is the top priority. The effective use and motivation of police officers often require department incentives (e.g., all levied fines returned to the police department budget) and special police units specifically assigned to bus priority enforcement.

Public Education Program and Posting of Fines Public education, including a close working relationship with abutting property owners, delivery services, and special transportation providers (e.g., taxicabs), is considered essential to successful bus priority operations in dense areas. Preliminary notification of all parties as to the fines for violations and the posting of the violations have effectively reduced enforcement requirements. In Seattle any violation of the exclusive bus lanes on 2nd and 4th Streets in the CBD is considered a moving violation with a more costly fine than that for nonmoving violations. Motorcycle officers are assigned along with patrolmen for enforcement and for pursuit of violators (P. Gilbert, Seattle Police Department; *personal communication*).

Heavy Initial Enforcement and Towing of Parked Vehicles Most successful bus priority projects have been supported by heavy initial enforcement. Both the New York and San Francisco projects relied heavily on extra initial enforcement provided by special civilian agents. Increased enforcement of commercial and passenger loading zones by means of rapid towing and impoundment is necessary to remove critical violations. In San Francisco, such improved enforcement of commercial loading and parking zones by the police resulted in over 1,800 cars being towed during the first month of the project (7).

Passive Enforcement and Travel-Time Penalty Posting a civilian agent at the cross street where right-turning vehicles are permitted to use the exclusive lane can force right turns to be made by vehicles using the lane. Motorists using the lane for other than right turns are forced to turn and thus encounter a travel-time penalty in their trip.

Special Enforcement on Opposite Curb Lane On one-way streets, parking violations on the curb opposite the bus lane rapidly deteriorate travel conditions both in the bus lane and in mixed traffic lanes. Enforcement thus involves the entire arterial roadway and is not limited only to the bus lane. In the Madison Avenue (New York City) project, special emphasis was placed on the enforcement of opposite curb parking restrictions.

Continuing Enforcement Experience with bus priority treatment has stressed the need for continuing enforcement. Violations tend to increase dramatically in periods of slack enforcement.

CONTRAFLOW BUS LANES

Usually a contraflow bus lane is a lane in the off-peak direction dedicated for the exclusive use of buses. This contraflow lane can be either the median lane for express bus service or the curb lane of a facility that otherwise carries one-way traffic. The latter is generally associated with CBD streets or other facilities on which frequent bus stops for passenger loading or unloading are anticipated. A special

FIGURE 8 Exclusive curbside bus lane in Washington, D.C., with van illegally using the lane.

FIGURE 9 A connector lane provides continuity between concurrent flow and contraflow segments of exclusive bus lane. *(Courtesy of American Public Transit Association.)*

type of contraflow lane is the reversible lane in which traffic is reversed daily to provide an additional lane in the peak direction without reducing the capacity of the off-peak direction.

Contraflow lanes on arterial roadways are generally operated only during peak hours. These lanes are usually used in the CBD; on one-way streets the curbside lane is almost always used. Interference by other traffic is minimal; however, signing requirements are extensive. Enforcement of contraflow lanes has been reported to be more easily accomplished than that of concurrent-flow lanes because, with proper signing, few motorists unintentionally venture into the lane (*8*, p. 11). Willful violators appear to be minimal.

Contraflow bus priority is more common in Europe than in the United States (*8*, p. 7). Paris has made extensive use of contraflow bus lanes with over 19 miles of this type of bus priority treatment in the central city and suburbs. Contraflow lanes are painted red and clearly marked; no physical barriers are used. Guidelines in Paris generally require at least one bus every 3 min to warrant designation of an exclusive bus lane.

More extensive design is required for contraflow lanes than for concurrent-flow lanes. Special lane designation is required, and traffic flow at the terminus of the bus lane must be carefully planned. Special signal phases may be necessary. Substantial operating costs are often encountered in the manual placing of stanchions for peak-period operation of contraflow bus lanes (*9*). Both concepts of contraflow lanes (peak-period operation on major arterials and 24-hr operation on one-way streets in the CBD) are discussed below.

Median Lane on Arterial Roadway

Often, urban arterial roadways leading to a major traffic generator, such as a CBD, have a distinct directional split; i.e., very high inbound volumes in the morning peak and very high outbound volumes during the evening peak. With such directional splits, unused capacity in the off-peak direction is available for exclusive bus lanes. In this approach to bus priority treatment, the median lane in the off-peak direction is used to provide an exclusive bus lane for the peak-period directional flow. Buses operate nonstop in the contraflow lane throughout its length. Careful design is required to permit ingress to and egress from the bus lane (Figure 9).

Specific design features for median lanes used for contraflow bus priority treatment are summarized in Table 2. Three significant design features for contraflow median lanes on urban streets should be noted. First, two traffic lanes should be available for vehicular traffic in opposing lanes. (Note the exception to the rule in the Kalanianaole Highway contraflow lane project discussed below.) Second, contraflow lanes and reversible lanes require extensive signing to preserve the integrity of the exclusive lane. Third, terminal points require special geometric design for safe and efficient traffic flow.

TABLE 2
FEATURES OF CONTRAFLOW BUS LANES

A. Median Lane on Arterial Roadway

Design Features

Lane Width	Design Speed[a]	Minimum One-Way Bus Volume	Practical Minimum Length	Roadway
12 ft	45–60 mph	40–60 buses/hr	Depends on bus routing and street geometrics (logical terminal points)	At least 2 lanes available for other traffic in opposing direction

Traffic Control Devices

Signing[b]				
Advance Warning	Restricted Lane	End of Bus Lane	Lane Demarcation	Special Markings
Roadside: R3–10 Overhead: R3–13 (see Figure 6)	Roadside: R3–11 Overhead: R3–14 (see Figure 6)	Roadside: R3–12 Overhead: R3–15 (see Figure 6)	Solid white line for bus-only lanes or 24-hr operation; broken white line for HOV lane and/or peak-hour-only operation	Diamond symbol on bus-lane pavement spaced so as to be in constant view by lane users

Restrictions

1. Hours of operation: Should operate throughout the day. Can operate during peak period only.
2. Turning movements: Prohibition of left turns by opposing traffic across bus lane during hours of priority operation.
3. Use of lane by other vehicles: Can be used by other HOV if not detrimental to express bus operation.

B. Curbside Lane on Arterial Roadway

Design Features

Lane Width	Design Speed[a]	Minimum One-Way Bus Volume	Practical Minimum Length	Roadway
20 ft desirable; 11 ft minimum	30–45 mph	20–30 buses/hr	2–3 city blocks (depends on geometrics)	At least 2 lanes available for other traffic in opposing direction (because lane width of 20 ft is desirable, parking should be prohibited at opposite curb)

Traffic Control Devices

Signing[c]				
Advance Warning	Restricted Lane	End of Bus Lane	Lane Demarcation	Special Markings
Roadside: R3–10 Overhead: R3–13 (see Figure 6)	Roadside: R3–11 Overhead: R3–14 (see Figure 6) (posted in each block as necessary)	Roadside: R3–12 Overhead: R3–15 (see Figure 6)	Solid white line for 24-hr bus operation (use of buttons or other delineators may increase awareness and aid enforcement)	Diamond symbol on bus-lane pavement spaced so as to be in constant view by lane users

Restrictions

1. Hours of operation: Continuous or during peak period only.
2. Turning movements: Left turns across contraflow bus lane are prohibited for opposing traffic. Buses operate with traffic-signal system so that no prohibition is necessary for cross-street traffic.
3. Use of lane by other vehicles: Taxicabs and commercial vehicles for loading and unloading may be permitted if lane width is sufficient to permit passing within the lane.

[a] Design speed for geometric design (this is greater than operating speed).
[b] Median Lane on Arterial Roadway: Reversible lanes require special signing and additional control devices. AASHTO recommends the use of overhead lane signals to control lane use on reversible lanes.
[c] Curbside Lanes on Arterial Roadway: Additional signs are necessary to warn pedestrians to look both ways before stepping off the curb.

Kalanianaole Highway (Oahu, Hawaii) Contraflow Bus Lane

An example of a contraflow lane on an arterial serving major traffic generators is the Kalanianaole Highway on the island of Oahu. Connecting the eastern portion of Oahu with downtown Honolulu and the University of Hawaii, the Kalanianaole Highway is a four-lane undivided arterial on which a contraflow lane was opened for 1.9 miles in August 1973. The inside lane of the opposing traffic was used for a 2-hr operation from 6:00 to 8:00 a.m. on weekdays. After 2 years of operation as an exclusive bus lane, the contraflow lane was opened to carpools with three or more occupants. At the end of the contraflow lane, the Kalanianaole Highway becomes a six-lane divided arterial, and the bus lane crosses the median for concurrent-flow for another 0.5 mile.

Operation of the contraflow lane permitted the 16 buses operating in the lane to make the inbound trip in 7 min, whereas other vehicular traffic required 10 min to make the same trip. Although bus patronage remained constant during the 4-year evaluation period, use of the lane by carpools increased significantly. Enforcement was not a significant problem; however, it was necessary to remove legal constraints for contraflow operation before implementation of the project (*10, 11*).

Madison (Wisconsin) Contraflow Bus Lane

A project in Madison, Wisconsin, provides an example of a contraflow lane that was discontinued due to lack of enforcement and the serious injury of a pedestrian. Operated for 13 years on a one-way couplet serving the CBD and the University of Wisconsin, the contraflow lane was discontinued in 1979 after unauthorized use of the lane by bicycles increased to the point that safety was a major problem. Over 300 bicycles per hour competed with the 40 buses per hour using the facility during peak periods. Enforcement did not prevent unauthorized use of the lane by bicycles, and the contraflow lane was closed, even though more efficient bus service had been provided. Buses currently operate in mixed flow on the one-way couplet (*12*).

Types of Violations

Three types of violations have been identified with contraflow bus priority in median lanes of arterials.

Illegal Left Turns and Crossing of Contraflow Lane The majority of traffic accidents on a contraflow bus lane are due to turning violations (*13*). (Accident rates on the total arterial facility tend to increase after installation of a contraflow bus lane, and severity of accidents also increases due to close proximity of opposing traffic.)

Unauthorized Use of Bus Lane Because of the reverse operation, violation rates by ineligible vehicles are normally low. (Unauthorized use of the contraflow median lane by bicycles is an exception to this condition.)

Unattentive Crossing of Contraflow Lane by Pedestrians Pedestrians often step into the contraflow lane while observing traffic in the opposite direction.

Effective Enforcement Strategies

In addition to the public education and marketing strategies applicable to most bus priority measures, enforcement measures for contraflow median lanes include good design to encourage self enforcement, adequate lane marking, and concentrated enforcement at intersections.

Geometric Design Features for Self Enforcement Good geometric design and heavy use by buses tend to make contraflow bus lanes self-enforcing. The design is often limited, however, by the existing street configuration.

Adequate Lane Markings and Proper Signing Adequate pavement markings and signs provide warnings to the nondeliberate violator. The placement of temporary stanchions, particularly at entrances to the contraflow bus lane, has proven to be effective in reducing violations.

Concentrated Enforcement at Intersections Concentrated enforcement can be provided at intersections with high accident rates in order to reduce illegal left turns. Potential violators can be warned and rerouted.

Curbside Lane on Arterial Roadway

The use of contraflow curbside lanes for bus priority operations is generally limited to one-way streets in a CBD or other dense development. Usually operated on a 24-hr basis, the lanes are often delineated by raised curbs. Heavy use of the lanes by buses make their special treatment obvious to the motorists and violations are rare. Parking violations within the lane are critical and jeopardize the priority operation.

Design features for contraflow curbside bus lanes are summarized in Table 2. The advantages of using a 20-ft-wide lane should be stressed. As buses cannot pass in the bus lane without encroaching in the lane of opposing traffic, a contraflow lane width that permits passing without leaving the lane is desirable.

Spring Street (Los Angeles) Contraflow Bus Lanes

The Spring Street contraflow bus lanes in Los Angeles provide an excellent example of contraflow curbside operation over a period of years and the design modifications resulting from an extensive evaluation. Opened originally in 1974 as a single curbside lane, contraflow operation was provided between Ninth and Macy Streets, a distance of 1.5 miles. However, the segment of the contraflow lane between

First and Macy Streets carries the heaviest volume of buses and, by 1979, problems were encountered in the transit operation. Many of the 1,145 buses that operated daily in the exclusive bus lane (260 buses in the 2-hr evening peak) encountered delays caused by bus-loading queues (all buses at City Hall had to wait until the first bus was loaded) and by difficulties in turning off to cross streets because of congestion. After an analysis in 1979, the original 13-ft-wide contraflow lane between First and Macy Streets was widened to 26 ft, bus-stop bypasses were initiated, local and express bus stops were separated, and new overhead warning signs were placed for better designation of the contraflow lane. A layout of the modified contraflow lane geometrics is shown in Figure 10. As a result of the modification, bus travel times were reduced by 20 percent during the evening peak period (*14*).

Second and Marquette Streets (Minneapolis) Contraflow Bus Lanes

In Minneapolis contraflow bus priority treatment is used on the curbside lanes of Second and Marquette Streets. Both facilities are heavily used by buses during the peak hour; over 75 buses use the contraflow lane on each street. Installation of the contraflow lanes has resulted in reduced travel times for buses through the CBD, even with high passenger pickup and discharge operations. Delivery trucks are permitted to use the lane except during peak periods.

The most common violation is that of stopping in the lane. Parking-meter control personnel are used during the peak period for continual enforcement of the bus lanes. Exits from parking garages cause significant enforcement problems during the peak periods, and many garages have employed off-duty patrolmen to assist in controlling exiting traffic. Additional enforcement problems were encountered with the increased use of vanpools, which used the opposite curb lane for pickup and delivery of passengers. Special emphasis was placed on locating vanpool collection and discharge points on cross streets (L. Boursell, Supervisor of Meter Monitors, City of Minneapolis; *personal communication*).

Types of Violations

Illegal parking, stopping, or standing in the contraflow lane are the most frequent violations and the most serious problems in causing bus delay (*15*). Each of these violations is a critical violation in that it seriously reduces the effectiveness of the bus lane. It should be emphasized that similar violations in the opposite curb lane also seriously affect the bus-lane operation and the total traffic flow. Other violations, such as illegal pedestrian and bicycle movements, common in contraflow median bus operation, are also prevalent in contraflow curbside bus facilities.

Effective Enforcement Strategies

Enforcement strategies, in addition to those previously identified for contraflow median lanes, include:

Use of Heavy Fines and Immediate Towing Procedures to Penalize Parked Violators See Brophy and Voccola (*16*), DiRenzo et al. (*17*), and Brophy (*18*) for descriptions of the extensive towing program in Washington, D.C.

Use of Meter Monitors for Peak-Hour Enforcement Meter monitors have been used effectively during peak periods for continual enforcement of the contraflow lane. Assessment of heavy fines or prompt towing can reduce the number of violations. Radio communication and standby tow trucks can facilitate vehicle removal.

BUS-ONLY STREETS AND AUTOMOBILE-RESTRICTED ZONES

Bus-only streets are generally implemented as part of CBD improvement projects. They tend to be located in areas of concentrated development and at the convergence of bus routes. Generally referred to as transit malls, bus-only streets serve as a major transit collection/distribution route and are integrated with pedestrian mall development. The primary objectives of transit malls are to provide increased transit accessibility and to separate different types of vehicles. While transit travel times are often increased in transit malls, the level of service for the entire system is improved through better passenger access and reduced loading time. Primarily because of the unique design and operation of transit malls, enforcement is usually not a problem.

An automobile-restricted zone (ARZ) is defined as a geographic area in which limitations are placed upon automobile use in favor of other modes. Similar to the transit mall, the ARZ is usually developed in conjunction with major central business district improvements. An ARZ is characterized by major geometric changes in the street network to give priority treatment primarily to pedestrians. Bus operations are also given priority to provide a substitute mode of travel for the banned automobile. A circulation system is developed within the ARZ to provide a framework for buses, taxis, and delivery trucks.

European cities have used the transit mall for a longer period of time than have cities in the United States. The earliest transit malls in the United States were Nicollet Mall in Minneapolis and 63rd and Holsted in Chicago. More recently, transit malls have been implemented in Philadelphia and Portland, Oregon (*8*, p. 13). In Boston an ARZ has recently been implemented in the CBD. Primarily for use by pedestrians, the ARZ provides circulation for buses and limited use by taxicabs and delivery vehicles (*19–21*).

Design guidelines for bus-only streets are summarized in Table 3. Because of the unique character of the ARZ, specific design guidelines are difficult to develop. However, general design criteria for roadway design are applicable both to

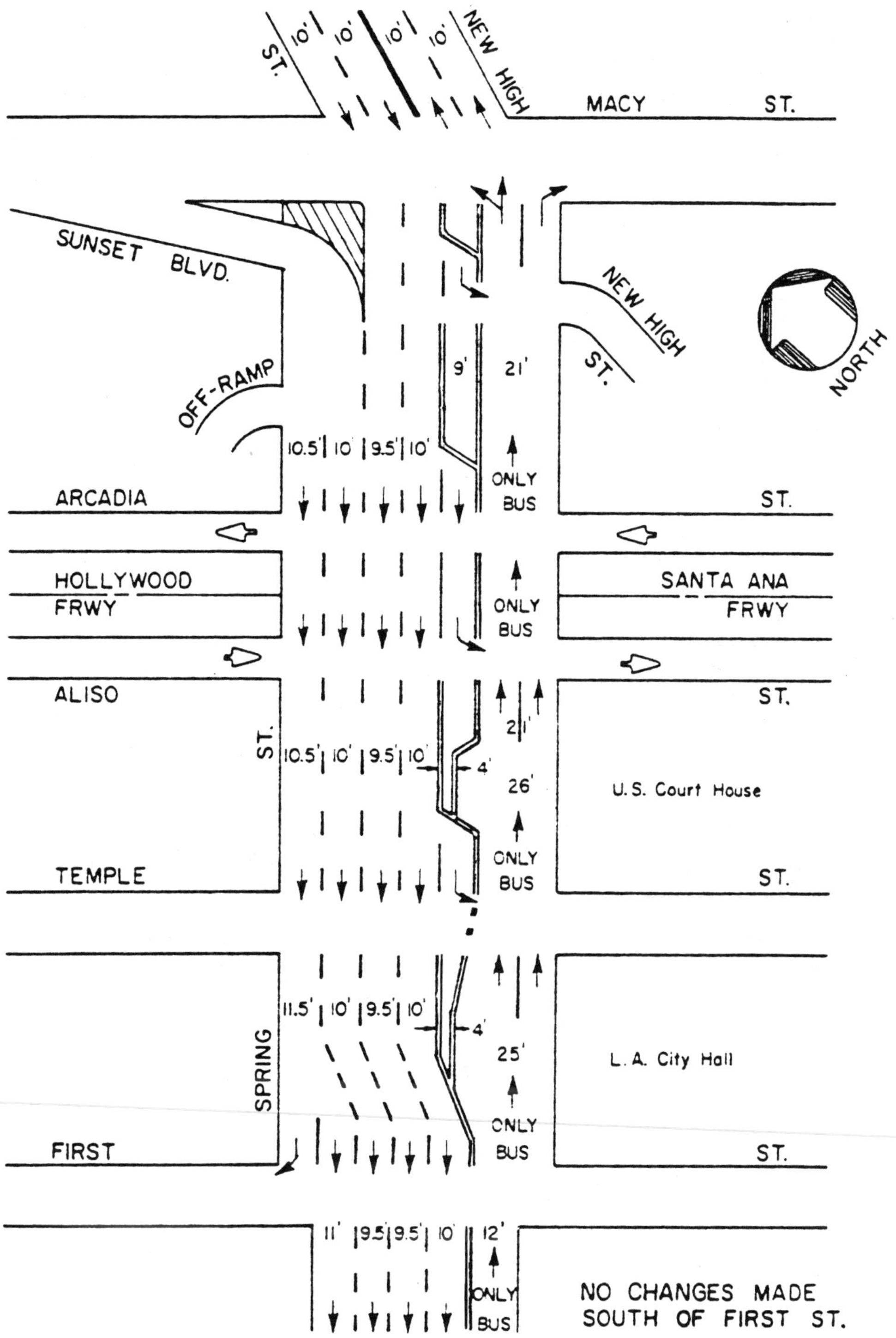

FIGURE 10 Revised Spring Street contraflow bus-lane configuration in Los Angeles, California.

TABLE 3
FEATURES OF BUS-ONLY STREETS AND AUTOMOBILE-RESTRICTED ZONES

Design Features

Bus-Only Street Lane Width	Design Speed[a]	Minimum One-Way Bus Volume	Practical Minimum Length	Roadway
Lane—12 ft Roadway—24 ft	15–25 mph	20–30 buses/hr	1 block (depends primarily on street pattern and system geometrics)	2-lane, 2-way roadway (transit malls are often designed with curvilinear roadway alignment)

Traffic Control Devices[b]

Signing				
Advance Warning	Restricted Lane	End of Bus Lane	Lane Demarcation	Special Markings
Roadside: R3–10 Overhead: R3–13 (see Figure 6)	Not required along bus-only street or within ARZ; no turns, R3–3 (MUTCD), for cross-street traffic	Roadside: R3–12 Overhead: R3–15 (see Figure 6)	Double yellow lines on bus-only lane if 2-way bus traffic is present	Pedestrian crosswalk pavement designation; warning signs for crossing pedestrian traffic

Restrictions

1. Hours of operation: 24 hr/day.
2. Turning movements: Right and left turns onto transit mall are prohibited.
3. Use of transit mall by other vehicles: Limited to bicycles and police vehicles. All private vehicles are prohibited. Taxis may use transit mall for pickup and delivery.
4. Special bus waiting areas (lay-bys) should be designed for project if heavy bus operations and bus transfers are anticipated.
5. In automobile-restricted zones, only bus and pedestrian traffic (and possibly taxi drop-off) is permitted. Special design is necessary to cordon off ARZ.

[a] Design speed for geometric design (this is greater than operating speed).
[b] Adequate traffic-control devices are often subordinated in transit malls in favor of aesthetics. Although there are minimal driver information requirements associated with a transit mall, standard traffic-control practices should not be compromised for a pleasing appearance.

bus-only streets and streets within ARZ's. Transit malls and ARZ's tend to be self-enforcing due to their design and the ease of identifying and apprehending violators.

Gothenburg, Sweden, Central Area

In Gothenburg, Sweden (population 450,000), automobile-restricted traffic cells have been effectively used in the central area. With a ring road to accommodate commuter and through traffic, the central area was subdivided in 1970 into five separate traffic cells, each encompassing several blocks. Borderlines between cells could be crossed only by emergency and public transit vehicles. Separate bus-only streets were provided outside the cells. Benefits included reduced noise and air pollution, a 50 percent reduction in the accident rate within the cells, an increase in transit ridership, and a 40 percent reduction in vehicle traffic (*4,* pp. 35–41).

Chestnut Street Transitway (Philadelphia)

The Chestnut Street Transitway in Philadelphia was developed in 1976 as part of the bicentennial celebration to improve transit operations and service to nearby major employment centers (Figure 11). The transit mall is 12 blocks long and consists of a two-lane, two-way roadway for buses. Automobiles are barred from the roadway; however, cross-street traffic is allowed. Taxis are permitted to use the mall to gain access to hotels. Midblock crossings have been constructed, and pedestrian amenities have been provided.

Studies conducted on transit travel times revealed little improvement over the previous conditions of mixed traffic. However, surveys indicated that environmental conditions, particularly levels of air and noise pollution, significantly improved with the development of transit mall. (*22, 23*).

Nicollet Mall (Minneapolis)

The Nicollet Mall in Minneapolis was developed in 1967 and extended in 1981. As a two-lane, two-way, curvilinear roadway, the mall carries between 45 and 60 buses in each direction in the peak hour. Access by automobiles is denied except for cross-street traffic. Pedestrian amenities are provided.

Buses operating on the mall travel at a faster speed than do those operating in mixed flow on parallel streets; however, they move at a slower speed than those operating in contraflow lanes on Second and Marquette Streets, primarily because of more frequent stops on the mall and a different ridership composition. Heaviest use of buses on the mall is during the lunch hour, indicating greater use of the mall by persons already in the CBD (*22*).

Types of Violations

Two types of violations have been identified in transit malls and ARZ's.

Unauthorized Use of the Transit Mall or ARZ

The violation rate is low as violators are highly visible and conspicuous. The curvilinear alignment of a transit mall and the geometric design at intersections with cross streets (principally turning radii) can make illegal turns onto the mall difficult. Truck delivery (if trucks are permitted to use the mall because other unloading areas are unavailable) is usually limited to off-peak hours; thus any violations by trucks are easily observed. Also heavy bus volumes during the peak hour discourage delivery trucks from using the mall.

Illegal Crossing by Pedestrians

This is the most common violation, but it is not a critical violation as bus travel is not usually interrupted by infrequent jaywalking. However, injuries to pedestrians have occurred due to casual crossing of the bus lanes without paying attention to traffic.

Effective Enforcement Strategies

Transit malls and ARZ's require little enforcement for effective operation. Enforcement of jaywalking violations becomes necessary only if bus flow is restricted by pedestrians. Police in Minneapolis, however, report that enforcement of jaywalking violations on the Nicollet Mall would be futile. Police patrolmen work intersections on the mall and their presence discourages pedestrian violations (*13, 22*).

SIGNAL PREEMPTION

Priority treatment for buses in mixed traffic flow can be achieved through signal adjustments in passive and active systems. Passive systems do not require special bus detection equipment; these systems are based on signal coordination and improved signal timing for all arterial traffic. Active systems utilize bus signal preemption capability and depend on adjustment of the signal phase to give priority to buses on the arterial facility (Figure 12). Significant benefits for bus priority have been reported when the two systems have been combined, i.e., effective signal coordination and bus signal preemption capability (*24*). Various other signal preemption techniques for bus priority operations have been used to control access to arterial roadways (*25*).

The objective of signal preemption by buses is to reduce bus travel time by means of fewer stops due to cross-street traffic. Bus delays at traffic signals have been reported to be 10 to 20 percent of overall bus trip times and the cause of almost one-half of all delays (*1*). The effectiveness of bus signal preemption in total movement of people is a function of the cross-street traffic. The greatest potential for signal

FIGURE 11 Chestnut Street Transitway bus mall in Philadelphia.

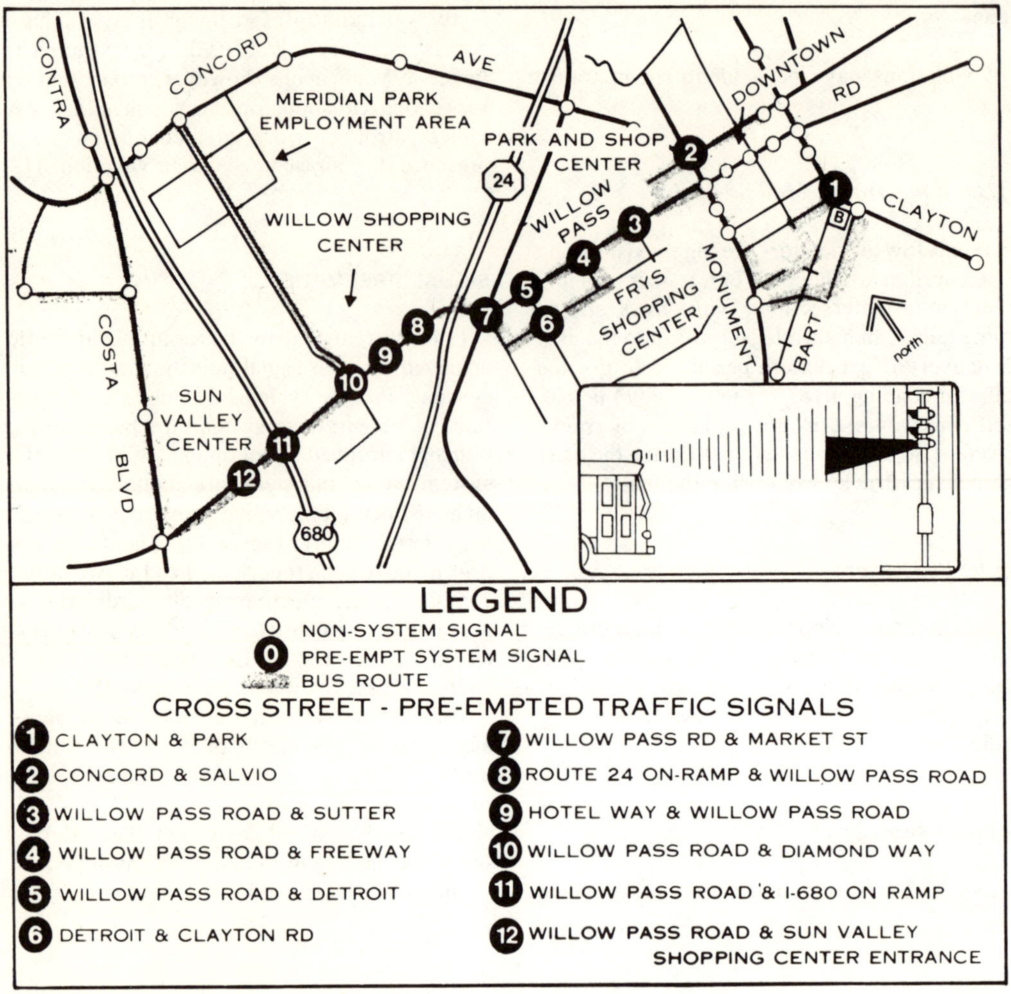

FIGURE 12 Map of Willow Pass corridor in Concord, California, which shows location of preempted traffic signals. *(Courtesy of American Public Transit Association.)*

preemption thus lies on arterial roadways with little cross-street traffic. Pedestrian clearance phases and progression on the cross streets must be considered as part of the total signal system operation in the use of signal preemption in a central business district.

Signal preemption by buses tends to be highly self enforcing inasmuch as normal and accepted signal control of traffic is involved. Few problems with enforcement have been reported in evaluations of signal preemption projects (*26*). Platoons of automobiles traveling around a bus to take advantage of the priority operation have been reported but are not considered a hazard or an enforcement problem. Perhaps the most significant problem is associated with bus drivers who anticipate a green signal and approach the intersection at a high rate of speed.

No special design features are required for signal preemption projects. Accepted AASHTO and MUTCD design guidelines are appropriate for arterial geometrics and traffic control devices.

Signal preemption is justified at an intersection when:

- Total person delay (a function of cross-street volumes) is reduced,
- At least 10 to 15 buses are carried on the arterial during the peak hour,
- A daily volume of at least 100 buses is carried, and
- The cross-street green phase can be reduced without conflicting with the minimum pedestrian clearance time.

The use of signal preemption in bus priority treatment has resulted in reduced bus travel times and smoother traffic flows on arterial streets. An evaluation of a 3.8-mile segment of Greenback Lane in Sacramento County, California, found a 24 percent reduction in bus travel times during peak hours when signal preemption was utilized on nine full-traffic-actuated signals. Increased overall bus speeds were due to reduced stopping time rather than reduced running time.

Types of Violations

Few violations have been specifically related to bus signal preemption. Possible violations include:

• Possession and use of the signal preemption transmitter by unauthorized persons.

• Running of red signals by motorists due to phase changes.

• Running of red signals by bus operators because of mistaken anticipation of a green phase.

Effective Enforcement Strategies

Bus signal preemption does not involve traffic operations significantly different than those encountered daily by motorists. Thus enforcement strategies beyond those normally employed for routine traffic enforcement are not required.

CONCLUDING REMARKS

Project design plays an important role in bus priority treatment on urban streets. If design is accomplished with enforcement needs in mind, not only can enforcement requirements be reduced, but also the project will tend to be self-enforcing. Project design must be considered within a perspective larger than merely geometric configurations. The design must carefully integrate transit operations, traffic engineering, and enforcement activities in a coordinated effort as part of the total program described in the preceding chapters. Project design must consider all phases of transit operations such as ridership demand, bus routing, accessibility to buses, and pedestrian traffic and apply acceptable design standards for traffic-control devices.

It should be emphasized that project design cannot substitute for a total program of enforcement, which must include public education, traditional enforcement techniques, and combined strategies for enforcement. However, it should be stressed that good project design, including sound geometric features and traffic-control devices, is a necessary element in priority bus operation, which includes enforcement, and cannot be replaced by an excess of public education or punitive measures for violations.

REFERENCES

1. LEVINSON, H. S., C. L. ADAMS, and W. F. HOEY. *NCHRP Report 155: Bus Use of Highways: Planning and Design Guidelines*. Transportation Research Board, Washington, D.C. (1975) 161 pp.
2. American Association of State Highway and Transportation Officials. *A Policy on Design of Urban Highways and Arterial Streets*. Washington, D.C. (1973)
3. Federal Highway Administration. *Manual on Uniform Traffic Control Devices*. U.S. Department of Transportation, Washington, D.C. (1978)
4. Public Technology, Inc. *Center City Environment and Transportation: Transportation Innovations In Five European Cities*. U.S. Department of Transportation, Washington, D.C. (1980) 59 pp.
5. ERIKSON, G. *Midpoint Status Report on Stockton Street Transit Improvements, Ten Month Demonstration*. (1981) p. 7.
6. COX, M. Reserved Bus Lanes in Dallas, Texas. *Transportation Engineering Journal,* No. TE4 (1975) pp. 691–704.
7. Public Technology, Inc. Some Lessons from San Francisco. *SMD Briefs 6* (July, 1981)
8. WILBUR SMITH and Associates. *Transit Preferential Streets Program—State of the Art Review*. Prepared for the City and County of San Francisco (1980)
9. MCCASLAND, W. R. Operational Evaluation of the I-45 Contraflow Lane. Draft Research Report 205–9. Texas Transportation Institute (1980)
10. Federal Highway Administration. *Evaluation of the Kalanianaole Highway Carpool/Bus Lane*. Report No. FHWA-RD-77-100. U.S. Department of Transportation, Washington, D.C. (1977)
11. ROTHENBURG, M. J. *Priority Treatment for High Occupancy Vehicles: Project Status Report*. Prepared for the Federal Highway Administration by JHK & Associates (1977)
12. BERG, W. D., R. L. SMITH, JR., T. W. WALSH, JR., and T. N. NOTBOHM. Evaluation of a Contraflow Arterial Bus Lane. Pp. 45–49 in *Transportation Research Record 798: Bus Planning and Operations*. Transportation Research Board, Washington, D.C. (1981)
13. MILLER, N. C., and R. B. DEUSER. *Enforcement Requirements for High-Occupancy Vehicle Facilities*. Report No. FHWA-RD-79-15. Federal Highway Administration, Washington, D.C. (1978)
14. City of Los Angeles Department of Transportation, Transportation Engineering Division; and Bus Planning Department, Southern California Rapid Transit District. *Evaluation of the Spring Street Contraflow Bus Lane Widening*. Prepared as part of the Southern California Association of Governments Overall Work Program (1980)
15. ERIKSON, G., W. E. HURRELL, and B. W. NELSON. Transit Lane Enforcement in the Central City. Pp. 75–82 in *Transportation Research Record 816: Transportation System Management—Parking, Enforcement, and Other Issues*. Transportation Research Board, Washington, D.C. (1981)
16. BROPHY, J. M., and H. W. VOCCOLA. Parking Enforcement and Follow Up. Paper presented at 25th Annual IMPC Conference, Hollywood, Florida, April 10, 1979.
17. DIRENZO, J. R., et al. *Study of Parking Management Tactics*. Volume 2. *Overview and Case Studies*. Report No. FHWA-PL-79-021. U.S. Department of Transportation, Washington, D.C. (1979)
18. BROPHY, J. Criteria for a Balanced Parking Program. Paper presented at the 23rd Annual Parking Workshop, Institutional and Municipal Parking Congress, June 8, 1977.
19. FAUTH, G. R., A. M. HOWITT, J. A. GOMEZ-IBANEZ, J. F. KAIN, and H. C. WILKINS. *Central Area Auto Restraint: A Boston Case Study*. UMTA-MA-11-0007-79-1 (1978) 264 pp.

20. LOUDON, W. R., W. M. PECHNOLD, and C. R. KERN (Cambridge Systematics, Inc.). *Boston Auto Restricted Zone Demonstration Evaluation Plan—Final Report.* UMTA-MA-06-0049-79-4 (1979)
21. ALGMIN, J. *Boston's Downtown Crossing: Its Effects on Downtown Retailing.* Boston Redevelopment Authority (1980)
22. CRAIN and Associates. *Streets for Pedestrians and Transit: An Evaluation of Three Transit Malls in the U.S.* PB 295278/OGA (1979)
23. LOUKISSOS, P. J., and R. GANCARZ. *Public Attitudes Toward Auto Restricted Streets in Philadelphia and Trenton.* Delaware Valley Regional Planning Commission, Philadelphia (1978)
24. WATTLEWORTH, J. A., K. G. COURAGE, C. E. WALLACE, R. S. WOLFE, and D. P. REAVES. *Evaluation of the NW 7th Avenue Express Bus and Bus Priority Systems.* Final Report I-1. Transportation Research Center, University of Florida, Gainesville (1978) 131 pp.
25. Transport and Road Research Laboratory. *Bus Demonstration Project. Summary Report No. 8 Southampton. A Linked System of Traffic Signals with Priority Access to the Route for Buses.* Department of the Environment, London (1976) 15 pp.
26. ELIAS, W. J. The Greenback Experiment. Signal Preemption for Express Buses: A Demonstration Project. California Department of Transportation, Sacramento County, Calif. (1976)

BIBLIOGRAPHY

Evaluation of Freeway High Occupancy Vehicle Lanes. Volumes I and II. Report No. DOT-P-80-30. U.S. Department of Transportation, Washington, D.C. (1980)

National Highway Institute. High Occupancy Vehicle Facility Development, Operation, and Enforcement (training course materials). Federal Highway Administration, U.S. Department of Transportation, Washington, D.C. (1981)

Public Technology, Inc. *Transportation System Management, Air Quality, and Energy Conservation.* A Report of the Transportation Task Force of the Urban Consortium for Technology Initiatives. U.S. Department of Transportation, Washington, D.C. (1980)

SCHWARTZ, S. I., A. HOLLANDER, C. LOUIE, and R. AMOROSO. Madison Avenue Dual-Width Bus Lane Project: Lessons for Other Areas. Paper presented at the Annual Meeting of the Transportation Research Board, Washington, D.C., January 1982.

WILBUR SMITH and Associates. *Sutter Post Geary O'Farrell Streets—Transit Preferential Streets Program.* Prepared for Department of City Planning, City and County of San Francisco (1981)